I0620890

Leaders of the Light in the Age of Great Awakening

Challenges and Opportunities Ahead

Don P. Valeri

B.A.(Hons.), LL.B,/J.D.,
M.B.A., Ph.D.

1st edition 2025

ISBN Paperback: 979-8-9990215-6-4
ISBN Hardcover: 979-8-9990215-7-1
Library of Congress Control Number: 2025919644

This book is dedicated to my daughter **Christa**, who has taught me so much and made my life worth living.

No father ever had a better daughter.

ACKNOWLEDGMENT

I would like to thank some very special luminous souls whose encouragement and teachings helped me develop spiritually and made this book possible: Royd Calvert, Petrina Bosiak, Zohra Venus Chaska Lucero, Laura Artuso, Maria Melo, and many other such souls I have met on my journey in this life.

3D Planet Earth Values	**5D Planet Earth Values**
Totalitarianism	Democracy
Top-down, pyramid organizations	Smaller flat organizations
Centralization	Decentralization
Competition	Cooperation collaboration
Focus on disease	Focus on health
Fear insecurity	Love compassion
War	Peace
Ecocide	Respect and nurturing nature
Poverty	Material abundance
Inequality	Egalitarianism
Empire building	Local and national sovereignty
Separateness	Inclusion
Ignorance	Wisdom
Religious dogma	Spiritual knowledge
Inorganic, synthetic technocracy	Organic, humanistic, alive

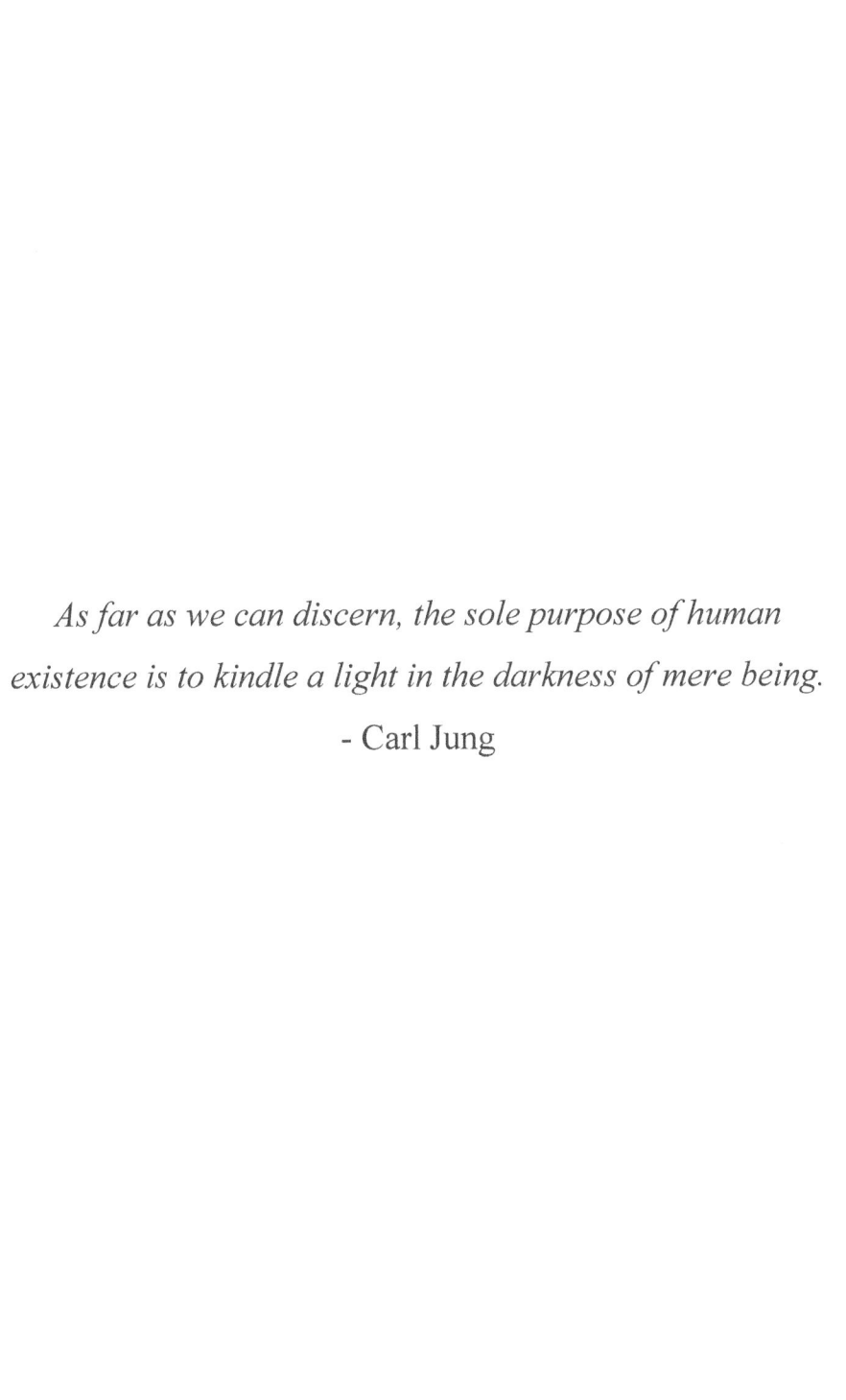

As far as we can discern, the sole purpose of human existence is to kindle a light in the darkness of mere being.

- Carl Jung

Contents

Chapter One 1

Introduction

Chapter Two.. 6

The Dark Side: Our Current Leaders And The World They Have Shaped

REFERENCES 49

Chapter Three.. 53

The Leader's Shadow: Friend Or Foe?

REFERENCES.. 71

Chapter Four 73

The Light Side

REFERENCES.. 103

Chapter Five 105

The Ethics And Moral Foundation Of A 5th Dimensional World

REFERENCES.. 118

CHAPTER SIX.. 119

A Lesson From The Past: Have We Been Here Before?

REFERENCES.. 135

Chapter Seven 137

Moral Imagination And Its Importance For Leaders Of The Light

REFERENCES.. 148

Chapter Eight.. 150

Conclusion

REFERENCES.. 166

About The Author

Chapter One

Introduction

"The time of Great Change is upon us, and is the outcome for those who embarked on a journey eons ago. All who have chosen to be here at this time are about to experience a transformation of a magnitude that few on earth can currently comprehend, and of which multitudes in the Universe regard in the highest esteem; the transformation of our Divine Mother Earth and the birthing of her Humanity into Beings of Light and Universal Creators."

George Kavassilas [1]

From its title, it might be thought this is a book about leadership in the 21st century. But that is not its true purpose. It is about the kind of leaders who will hopefully emerge in the coming years and decades, if humanity is to survive on this planet. Moreover, a great many changes will have to occur before these *leaders* will come forward.

It has been said in the Bible that "by their fruits ye shall know them." Look then at the 'fruits' of our current 'leaders' representing the ruling elites of the planet. In 2008, the world economy nearly imploded as a result of a financial meltdown on Wall Street. We have ongoing wars, at the time this is written, in the Ukraine, Israel,

---

[1] George Kavassilas, Our Universal Journey (Adelaide, Australia, Our Journey Home, 2012), p.250.

Africa, and elsewhere, consuming trillions of dollars of wealth and the loss of hundreds of thousands of lives and massive property destruction. Large corporations continue to poison and pollute our lands, the sea, and the sky. The entire world's population was put under medical house arrest based on faulty science, aided and abetted by Big Pharma corporations that profited in the billions and was able to direct the World Health Organization to do its bidding. Many countries are devolving into Mad Max scenarios. All of these 'fruits' are being done in order to feed the greed, selfishness, and short-term visions of our elites. The verdict is simple and stark: our political, economic, social, military, and educational Malthusian elites have proven themselves to be morally, intellectually, and financially bankrupt.

The vast majority of these so-called leaders are appointees and rarely, if ever, held accountable for their "fruits". The truth emerging is that they have lost the confidence of the majority of the world's population. They are no longer held in esteem or awe. As leadership scholar Jean Lipman-Blumen has put it, in this interdependent world, autonomous, authoritarian decisions, favored by traditional leaders, are no longer feasible or acceptable. Interdependence and diversity demand an empathic understanding and recognition of overlapping problems, mutual needs, and entwined destinies.[2]

The foregoing analysis points to a leadership crisis. It does not, however, suggest a new way forward, which is what this work is really about. This will necessitate a new species of leaders. Some of the traits of these new "leaders" to be looked at include empathy, authenticity, and emotional and mental balance. Those characteristics will play a significant role in the

---

[2] Jean Lipman-Blumen, "Connective Leadership," in Political and Civic Leadership: A Reference Handbook, ed. Richard A. Couto (Los Angeles, Sage Reference, 2010), p. 772.

21st century. But they will not alone lead humanity to a 5th-dimensional consciousness. Such a dimension would look and feel much differently than our current largely 3rd to 4th dimensional one. In this dimension, human consciousness will reflect values such as manifesting from the heart and not the head or ego, telepathy, creative mastery and expression, co-operation as opposed to competition, less density and a lighter body, telepathic experiences, wisdom, abundance, thriving, and unconditional love. It will be a world where people live more harmoniously and joyfully in a unity consciousness. From today's perspective, this world seems quixotic, ephemeral, and a fantasy. For sure, the ground we stand on now is decades and several generations away from a 5th-dimensional consciousness. This work is about what must change for this to happen. If you look closely, you can see signs of this change already germinating and emerging. So far, only saints, Mystics, esoteric philosophers, metaphysicians, and a small number of advanced, "older" souls have envisioned what this world will look like. In the coming years, they will be joined by millions of souls who have awakened.

To discuss the new "leaders" of the 21st century are eight chapters. Chapter two deals with the dark side and will not be pleasant reading for those looking for positivity, creativity, and illumination. To understand where we are now, one must know how we got here. One needs to understand why certain people became our rulers who bear enormous responsibility for the state of our planet. If you know very little about psychopathy, you will find this analysis one of the best explanations of the current malaise and leadership crisis. What does a psychopath and his close cousin, the sociopath, look like? How is it that so many psychopaths end up at the top of the pyramid? His or her absence of a conscience, obsession with power, and lack of empathy are compelling reasons why they behave the way they do.

This chapter will be followed by a short chapter dealing with the 'shadow' work, which every person has to do and learn from and transcend if they wish to evolve spiritually. For a 'leader', it is an absolute sine qua non. Anyone who aspires to play a leadership role in our communities must do this work. If they haven't, then they cannot be trusted and can cause enormous damage. It is patently obvious that humanity needs a better class of leaders, women and men of a different breed, of non-psychopathic, non-sociopathic, and non-narcissistic natures. To get them, enormous social, political, psychological, and educational changes must take place. Hopefully, a natural aristocracy of virtue and talent can emerge. They will have some idea of what natural law is and will be guided by a conscience and a moral compass. Our survival as a species will depend on these transformations.

Chapter four is the cornerstone of this work. It deals with leaders of the *Light* upon whom the Great Awakening has waited for and will rely upon in order to unfold. They are more balanced humans, not the left-brain dominant humans who have taken over the reins of power in our modern world. We will come to recognize what Iain McGilchrist has said, that a psychopath is someone with a severe right hemisphere dysfunction and whose brain is steeply skewed to the left. Light leaders will demonstrate greater levels of warmth, sociability, agreeableness, trust, straightforwardness, altruism, modesty, and tender-mindedness, amongst other qualities.[3] The qualities of whole-brain, balanced hemispheres will make a massive difference in societal outcomes. The concept of 'fractal leadership' will be introduced, and some ideas of what a 5th-dimensional world will look like will be introduced.

---

[3] Iain McGilchrist, The Matter with Things, Volume 2 (London; Perspectiva Press, 2021), p. 1346.

Having introduced what a 5th Dimensional civilization might look like, the obvious question any student of history will pose is: has there ever been such a civilization? The answer to this question may surprise some readers. Yes, there has. But proving that with tangible evidence is problematic. This chapter will deal with the issues and parameters of that possibility, what it could have looked like, and what lessons it holds for us today.

Given the presumption that such a civilization can evolve, it is necessary that its ethical foundation be explored. Without an ethical structure, no society can ever survive for long. A chapter will be devoted to the ethical tenets, principles, and building blocks of a 5th-dimensional civilization. This will be in contrast to the unethical, amoral milieu that permeates so much of our modern technological civilizations.

A chapter on moral imagination is included to expand on the theme of an ethical structure of a 5th-dimensional civilization. Every 5D leader will have this quality, permitting him or her to be visionary and fully expressed.

The concluding chapter will discuss the social, political, legal, and economic impediments to a 5th Dimensional civilization ever coming to fruition. It will point to the possibility that prior to these impediments ever being overcome, a change and rise in human consciousness will and must take place. It will sweep aside these hurdles and in a manner and speed that will shock many. This change in human consciousness is already beginning to emerge and, like an idea whose time has come, it offers humanity hope and optimism. It was Lenin who said, for decades, nothing happens, then in a matter of weeks, decades happen. One can hope we see this take place, but hopefully with a different ending than the one Lenin helped bring about.

Chapter Two

The Dark Side: Our Current Leaders And The World They Have Shaped

One does not become enlightened by imaging figures of light but by making the darkness conscious.
Carl Jung, "The Philosophical Tree" (1945/1954) CW 13, 335.

Introduction:

It is more or less obvious to most intelligent and perceptive people that we are in the midst of a period or epoch of rapid transformation from one type of society, even civilization, to another. Futurists, economists, psychics, and others have no real clear idea what will unfold during the next decade, let alone the century. Some have described this transformation as a revolution or even a war. No matter how it is described, the question will remain: Who will be our leaders? What will they look like in the years ahead? Will they be any different from our current crop of mostly incompetent, corrupt, sociopathic, dysfunctional, mentally ill sycophants?

The term 'leader' here is used guardedly and cautiously. It does not mean what most people think it means. Two academic writers, and others, namely Gary Gemmill and Judith Oakley, have put forth the argument or hypothesis that leadership is an

6

alienating social myth.[1] It is a myth that reinforces existing social mores and habits that rely on and necessitate hierarchy and the current dysfunctional expression of leadership. It has led to the devolution of leadership as a social process reflected in the obsolescence, decay, and destructiveness of so many social, political, and economic institutions. So, people keep asking now more than ever, 'Who and where are our leaders?' The answer depends in part on whether inorganic or organic leaders emerge. The focus of this work will be more on the "leader" than leadership, as an analytical approach. Hundreds of definitions of 'leadership' have proliferated in the last half century. Even an attempt to come up with a 'general theory of leadership' by leadership scholars has come up short. On the other hand, people generally know and can recognize a 'leader' when they see one.

The roots of this dichotomy can be traced to the Manichean Zoroastrian formula of cosmic duality, which the Hebrew prophets and early Christians depicted as the Sons of Light versus the Sons of Darkness, which will be discussed later in this work. We are talking about a class of people who do not believe in leadership as it is commonly understood. They have made it clear, if you look closely at how they act, that 'leadership' to them is a tool used to manipulate, confuse, and mislead followers. What they really mean is 'rulership'. They have become the Sons of Darkness.

They are the 'rulers' and everybody else is the 'ruled'. Leadership to them is about rulership: Who are the rulers? How do they become rulers? How do they maintain their rulership? This mentality and set of values allow the few to control the many. Now, when the few control the many, for it to be a sustainable, fruitful, and positive experience for us, then the few must either be benevolent dictators or a true aristocracy, a government by the best, as perhaps

---

[1] Gary Gemmell and Judith Oakley, "Leadership: An Alienating Social Myth?" Human Relations, 45 (2) (1992), 113-129. The citation.

Aristotle understood it. Modern thinkers like Thomas Jefferson and Thomas Paine also envisioned a 'natural aristocracy', based on talent, virtue, and real-world work experience. Historically, once in a while, a benevolent dictator will emerge, but rarely a natural aristocracy that lasts long.

It is important to point out that the 'rulers' are more often than not an 'invisible' class. Today, they are pushing the 'New World Order' by capturing movements and financial institutions. In previous cultures, they were more exposed, surrounded by their courtiers, warlords, aristocratic families, bankers and financial supporters, and sycophants. This was most obvious during the age of the monarchies, which entered a very steep decline during and after the French Revolution in 1789-1792. Everyone could see the king, even if he had no clothes on. From that time to now, these invisible, corrupt ruling classes did more and more to hide in the shadows, behind a veil of ignorance, which was much easier when education was so poor and communication between people so limited and restricted. Even today, few people understand the power of the financial elites and the tiny top 1%, who control the planet. They have played a major role in causing recessions and depressions, including the most recent Covid one, which was caused by massive lockdowns and supply chain interruptions. Benjamin Disraeli, former Prime Minister of Great Britain in the 19th century, correctly put it, "The world is governed by very different personages from what is imagined by those who are not behind the scenes."

Broadly speaking, at an organizational level, there can be distinguished two types of 'leaders'. One group is known as 'managers' and is not really true leaders, as discussed in this work. It is familiar to anyone who has studied the field of management, as most business, finance, and accountants are required to do. But, what, in fact, is a manager? What does he or she do? How can they be distinguished from 'leaders' with whom so many confuse them?

From a military and management perspective, the distinction between what leaders and managers do has been well articulated by Second World War General Sir William Slim:

"...We in the Army do not talk of 'management' but of 'leadership'. This is significant. There is a difference between leaders and managers. [Leadership represents] one of the oldest, most natural, and most effective of all human relationships. [Management is] a later product, with neither so romantic nor so inspiring a history. Leadership is of the spirit, compounded by personality and vision; its practice is an art. Management is of the mind, more a matter of accurate calculation of statistics, of methods, time tables, and routine; its practice is a science. Managers are necessary; leaders are essential."[2]

Other differences include: management is about path following; leadership is about path finding. Management is about doing things right; leadership is about doing the right things. Management is about planning and budgeting; leadership is about establishing direction. Management is about controlling and problem solving; leadership is about motivating and inspiring.[3]

Managers focus on systems, structure, and control, take a short-range view, imitate, accept the status quo, and are the classic 'good soldiers'. Leaders innovate, develop, transform, create, focus on people, inspire trust, take a long-range perspective, originate, challenge the status quo, and are his or her own person.[4]

----

[2] Roger Gill, Theory and Practice of Leadership (Second Edition), Sage Publications, p. 16.
[3] Ibid. p. 26.
[4] Ibid. p. 26.

What's often overlooked is that when many people talk of a leader, they are really thinking of a manager. Though they may or may not have had any input into a decision, managers are told what the decision will be. Being a leader requires a person to have the courage to do the right thing even if it is not the popular thing to do. Most importantly, leaders have the courage to introduce change into and through an organization or social structure. This can be very risky, and one reason managers often shirk from this challenge. The life span of a leader is often very short and can end in some form of assassination or termination from within by saboteurs, obstructionists, and change resisters. Think of the fate of Lincoln, Gandhi, John and Robert Kennedy, Martin Luther King, Malcolm X, and many others. Not even a public trial will always save them (Socrates, Jesus, Joan of Arc). It is much safer to be a manager.

The Leadership Myth Explanation:

The foregoing discussion is what mainstream, established thinking has had to say about 'leadership' in the current world we live in. A fifth-generation society, however, will not necessarily conform to its parameters and ideas as a completely new paradigm of values will emerge. Gary Gemmell and Judith Oakley, and others have pointed out that this mainstream thinking is based on an illusion. Humanity has been indoctrinated by a set of deeply ingrained cultural assumptions. Chiefly, humans have been taught that "leaders" are unquestionably necessary for the function of organizations and, therefore, society as a whole. This assumption is predicated on the belief and faith in hierarchies. However, this social construct of 'leadership' can easily be viewed as a myth when analyzed objectively. The myth reinforces so many social beliefs and structures that no one ever questions, except for anarchists and fringe thinkers. Through a social process of reification, this social construction of leadership is mystified and given an objective, real-world existence. It has become what Erich Fromm has described as a 'false consciousness', or what the content of the conscious mind that is fictitious and has been assimilated without our awareness. We are victims of Plato's cave analogy, looking at shadows and believing they are real. Through cultural programming and conditioning, this reification serves to meet various unconscious emotional needs of people who believe, uncritically and perhaps naively, that they cannot survive without a leader, someone who tells them what to believe and what to do.[5] This may also have its roots in our tribal lives thousands of years ago, when every tribe had a head of the clan or family, often the fiercest warrior, successful hunter, wise person, or shaman.

As Gemmell and Oakley have put it, "when people and members of a group are faced with uncertainty and ambiguity, regarding direction, they often report experiencing feelings of anxiety, helplessness, discomfort, disappointment, hostility, and fear of failure. Frightened by these emerging emotions and impulses, which are ordinarily held in check by absorption into the prevailing social system, they collude largely unconsciously to dispel them by projecting onto 'leadership' or the 'leader' role. The projection allows organizational members to avoid directly confronting the emerging emotions and regress to a social order that they are familiar with."[6] These social defences can produce mindlessness, induce massive learned helplessness, and mass formation psychosis. The 2019-2022 'covid' pandemic is a perfect example. The massive learned helplessness has been characterized by feelings of despair and resistance to any alternative form of action that has not been prescribed by the medical establishment and Big Pharma. As it has become apparent that the covid vaccines could not stop the 'virus' or prevent its transmission, the faith of many people in our leaders has been shaken. The possibility of alternative, cheaper treatments,

---

[5] Gemmell and Oakley, pp.113-114.

[6] Ibid. p.114.

known all along and used successfully in many third-world countries, has become increasingly obvious. The danger here is that as the despair and helplessness deepens, the search and wish for a messiah, magical rescue leaders, or even fascist draconian laws begin to accelerate.[7] There is a natural social tendency for people to give up their personal power and sovereignty and surrender to the myths of leadership, the need for a great leader to rescue us. In over-idealizing the 'leader', people deskill themselves from their own critical thinking, visions, inspirations, and emotions, rather than ratchet up and elevate their skills. This passivity opens the doors for the 'rulership' elites to take power and enforce their visions, rules, thinking, and values, which are anything but democratic.

One way to recognize this process is to detect the fabrication of fictions as illusions. These fictions are funnelled into people's consciousness through the media and the educational systems, which are mostly government-controlled. They work almost unrecognizably to prevent an awareness of an alternative reality that might threaten the existing natural order. Think of the covid contraction and death rates of people dying from the covid 'virus', which were distorted by false positive results from PCR tests. Hundreds of thousands of reported covid deaths were really deaths from comorbidities.[8] In the words of John Lamb Lash, the human race has been subjected to biophobia in the pandemic scam that condemns breathing as a public crime and makes every living person into a bioweapon.[9] Because the social fiction of the 'leader' is inculcated outside

---

[7] Ibid. p.115.

[8] The opinions here have been expressed by many learned and knowledgeable experts: Dr. Robert Malone, Dr. Peter McCullough, Dr. Joseph Mercola, Peter R. Breggin M.D., Robert F. Kennedy Jr., and many other awakened souls.

[9] John Lamb Lash, Not in his Image, London, Chelsea Green Publishing (2021), p. 341.

the awareness of followers, reality testing is blocked and the development of genuine insight into social issues, such as the covid 'scamdemic,' is undermined.[10]

There are many such fictions that people are deceived by: government of the people for the people, by the people; the common good; the sovereignty of the people; the great leader myth (an omnipotent and magical ideal person who has never ever lived); the divine right of kings; even the very conceptualization of the leader and the people. The greatest fiction may be that the people, or their representatives, can actually become 'leaders'. This misconception was well expressed by English philosopher David Hume in 1758, and truth be told, it applies equally today:

> "Nothing is more surprising to those who consider human affairs with a philosophical eye, than to see the easiness with which the many are governed by the few; and to observe the implicit submission which men resign their own sentiments and passions to those of their rulers. When we inquire by what means this wonder is brought about, we shall find that Force is always on the side of the governed; the governors have nothing to support them but opinion. 'Tis therefore, an opinion that government is founded; and this maxim is extended to the most despotic and most military governments, as well as to the most free and democratic."[11]

So, it is true also of income, wealth, and power, which are in the hands of the few and at the expense of the many. For example, today, at this writing, 90% of all stock held in the U.S. is in the hands of only 10% of families.

---

[10] Gemmell, and Oakley, p.117.

[11] Edmund S. Morgan, Inventing the People, New York, W.W. Norton, 1988, p.13.

When referring to the role of money in this process, Charles Hugh Smith, a prolific writer on our economy, technology, and social innovation, has had this to say:

> In the modern era, money is issued by governments or their central banks, and this control is imposed by force: if you violate the currency laws, you will be prosecuted and imprisoned.

> In other words, our social construct is a *manifestation of power:* the government demands that we use its currency, which it creates and distributes in a process that concentrates income, wealth, and power in the hands of the few at the expense of the many. This result is not a random side-effect of our monetary system – *it is the core feature of our monetary system.* There is actually no other possible output of the way our system creates and distributes money other than rising wealth and income inequality.

> The asymmetry of outcomes (the wealthy and powerful get richer and everyone else competes for crumbs) explains why the monetary system must be enforced by the State: if the system benefited all equally, everyone would choose to use it out of self-interest. There would be no need for the State to enforce the system on its citizens… The saying good ideas don't require force expresses this principle: ideas that are self-evidently fair and just will be adopted voluntarily. Only intrinsically unfair and unjust ideas must be enforced, as they reward the few at the top of the wealth-power pyramid at the expense of everyone below.[12]

The wealthy few also have tremendous political power because they are the only ones who can afford to make large political campaign contributions and buy (or bribe) all the other accoutrements of political favoritism. Additionally, we live in a current world system that is really an arrangement set up to

---

[12] Charles Hugh Smith, <u>Money & Work Unchained</u>, Berkeley, California, Oftwominds, 2017, p. 144.

allow a privileged minority to externalize nearly all their costs onto the rest of society, while pocketing as much as possible of the benefits themselves.[13] As Thomas Piketty and others have pointed out, the primary source of wealth inequality is a situation where capital (return on capital) is higher than the overall rate of economic expansion of the economy.[14] So the profits generated by the holders of capital are not real profits. They are accounting or bookkeeping fictions. They are gains reaped by passing production costs (current and future) on to everyone else.[15] And the larger the enterprise, the more likely and easier this is to do. How? Via the collusion of the state and private capital. The state and the elites depend on high profits (e.g., from a rising stock market) for their own revenues/wealth. They do this by placing their future costs of production (air pollution that must be remedied, rising future health care costs, drained aquifers, poisoned water and soil, contaminated toxin laden food, disappearance and destruction of habitats, as well as decimation of animals, insects and fisheries) onto the rest of society (i.e. the people). If they had to pay for all of these costs as they go, their profits would be reduced even decimated, or eliminated, unless they had the technology to remedy their production processes in place prior to production.[16] This is one of the chief reasons the elites must maintain their control of governments at all costs and allow the fiction of 'democracy' to continue.

There is also another class of persons who benefit from this oligarchic system, in which the many are ruled by the few: well-educated, mobile professionals and managers with secure incomes and abundant opportunities to gain recognition and build social capital. They belong to a class that is more equal than others and are able to benefit from the system's inequalities. They like to think of

---

[13] Charles Hugh Smith, Inequality and the Collapse of Privilege, Berkeley, California, Oftwominds, 2016, p.55.
[14] Ibid. p.55.
[15] Ibid. p.55.
[16] Ibid. p.55.

themselves as 'leaders.' They are not real leaders or what that term refers to here. At most, they are the managers of the managers beneath them in the pyramid. It is natural for these well-educated to project their satisfaction in the system to everyone else: "I am doing well because the system works great. You are not doing well because there is something wrong with you; their experience of the system is limited to their peer group at the top, who benefit at the expense of the many.[17]

Below this class are the many workers and labourers, who are alienated from their work by the profit-maximizing market. Generally speaking, their honesty, diligence, trust, and sincerity are exploited in the service of maximizing the profits of the few. Their only real refuge is through conscious or political movements that seek to change the draconian punitive laws governing them. And the only real possible solution to this inequality is to distribute political power and opportunities to build capital in a non-politicized (i.e., non-State) decentralized system that cannot be hijacked by vested interests or the State. Hence, the use of State welfare to substitute for 'bread and circuses' is not a long-term viable solution. The various layers of human community, reciprocity, obligations, duty, the joy of sharing, and sacrifice are marginalized by the State because individuals are paid directly by the State and not because of their actions or efforts on behalf of others, but simply because they are drawing breath. In the impersonal system of State-issued welfare, there is no need to recognize the needs of others, to share tasks that benefit all or make any sacrifices in the spirit of reciprocity; instead, the State meets all the needs of the individual without demanding anything in exchange except dependence on the State and the totalitarian requirement to pay enormous taxes. In a real sense, State welfare is not only anti-social but profoundly inhumane. Once the individual has been

---

[17] Ibid. p.74.

reduced to dependence on the State, he or she is atomized, non-resistant, passive, complicit, and compliant.[18] Any resistance to the State raises the threat of being cut off from the State's largesse. This is how a welfare state starves its recipients of social and human capital, innovation, and initiative, which are the very assets needed to assemble the wealth-creating capital to escape poverty.[19] Hence, both the individual and the community are reduced as threats to the State and the 'few' who control it.

Additionally, a debt-based monetary system only aggravates this situation exponentially. Is it any wonder that the only possible outputs of such a society are exploitation, alienation, the destruction of the human ties that create communities, and the rise of anti-social pathologies?[20] All one needs to do is look at the fate of many rust belt cities and communities in the U.S., such as Detroit, Michigan.

So far, from an organizational perspective, any discussion of 'leadership' has to be able to distinguish 'management' activities from what are colloquially referred to as 'leadership' functions. They are not the same and are nearly completely and confusedly lumped together. Many of the skills and attributes of managers have been identified as expressions of 'leadership'. In this work, the latter term has a more discreet and focused meaning, despite the overlap of the two activities. Thus, a very skilled manager can also be a 'leader' in certain circumstances. What then distinguishes a 'leader' from a manager? There are literally thousands of books and articles that enunciate hundreds of different definitions of 'leadership'. The main distinction being suggested here is that a 'leader' is someone who instigates and promotes, and motivates *change*. This is a very risky undertaking. Hundreds of years ago Machiavelli put it in <u>The Prince</u> as follows: "It ought to be remembered that there is nothing more

----

[18] Ibid. p.74
[19] Ibid. p.75.
[20] Ibid. p.76.

difficult to take in hand, more perilous to conduct, or more uncertain in its success, than to take the lead in the introduction of a new order of things, because the innovator has for enemies all those who have done well under the old conditions, and lukewarm defenders in those who may do well under the new." Clearly, Machiavelli was speaking here of extra-organizational contexts such as provincial or national political arrangements. But this insightful observation is also applicable to intra-organizational dynamics.

Up to this point, two different classes of 'leadership' have been discussed: managers qua leaders, and fictitious 'leaders'. There is, however, a third class of leadership, hitherto and universally known as "rulers". Today, that term is rarely heard in Western democratic or quasi democratic societies. It smacks of monarchy or autocratic regimes governed by dictators, even though there have been benevolent rulers from time to time, usually brought about by 'enlightened and responsible' elites.

It might be useful to look at the roots or etymology of the word 'lead'. It can be traced back over a thousand years to the old English word *leden* or *laedan*.[21] It meant to guide or show the way. Some etymologists have traced the word 'leadership' to around 1834, when the verb was converted into a noun. As this writer has argued elsewhere, both of these terms were understood to mean what they mean today, but not expressed as they are today with these words.[22] You can read the writings of the ancient Greeks and Romans, as well as the ancient Chinese philosophers, and rarely do you ever see the word 'leadership'. What you see are the words 'ruler' and 'rulership'.

This distinct ancient understanding of 'leaders and leadership' was very clearly expressed by Xenothon (430 – 354

---

[21] Chambers, Dictionary of Etymology, (1988), p. 584.

[22] Don Valeri, The Origins of Servant Leadership, (2007).

BC), a contemporary of Socrates and Plato in ancient Greece. Management guru, Peter Drucker, once commented that if you wished to learn about leadership, you must read Xenothon. One of his works, The Cyropaedia, relates a fictional life, perhaps history, of Cyrus the Great, the founder of the first Persian Empire. Xenophon emphasizes Cyrus' virtues and leadership qualities, which kept the Persian Empire together. It is a story of how an autocratic, all-powerful 'ruler' should conduct themselves as a 'ruler'. It has undoubtedly influenced many would-be monarchs or emperors who received a classical education. Unfortunately, few such 'rulers' have been able to emulate Xenophon's Cyrus very well.

Xenophon's other famous work on 'leadership' is The Anabasis. This is an autobiographical retelling of Xenophon's experience in Persia when he joined 10,000 Greek mercenaries in a military campaign supporting Cyrus the Younger in his war against Tissaphernes, a Persian satrap. Cyrus is killed in battle, and the 10,000 Greek mercenaries are left without generals and commanders, who were lured into a trap by the Persians and slaughtered. The Persians believed that without officers and commanders ('leaders'), the Greeks would fall apart and be easy to subdue and destroy. After all, they were deep in hostile territory, thousands of kilometres from home, surrounded by a hostile population. In reaction to their dire predicament, the Greeks elected new leaders from among their ranks, one of whom was Xenophon. Under his management and guidance, the ten thousand marched north to the Black Sea and eventually made it back to Greece. They were in effect a 'marching democracy.'

It's been said that the origin of democracy can be traced to ancient Athens, the city in which Xenophon, Socrates, and Plato lived in the 4th century BC. The vivid contrast that Xenophon paints in the Cyropaedia and the Anabasis is noteworthy for numerous reasons. The path of 'rulership' is laid out in the former, and that of 'democratic leadership' in the latter. For centuries, the former model has been triumphant. Though a republic emerged in Rome and again in many Medieval city states and Germanic "free towns", it was not until the American and French Revolutions that more 'democratic' models of 'leadership' emerged. Historian Edmond S. Morgan describes this social and political transformation: "The word 'leader' is old, but 'leadership' was a term that no one seems to have felt a need for as long as the qualities it designates remained an adjunct of social superiority. The decline of deference and the emergence of leadership signalled the beginnings not only a new rhetoric but of a new mode of social relations and a new way of determining who should stand among the few to govern the many. It signalled not only the rise of the professional politician and religious hero but the vulnerability of any institution that denied the equality in which men and women had been created."[23]

What Morgan has not quite articulated is that those few, in order to maintain their positions as 'leaders', created a new fiction or myth called 'leadership'. This was done to reinforce existing social beliefs and structures about the necessity of hierarchies and 'leaders' in organizations. One method of doing this is to promote the idea that people are basically stupid and evil and cannot live in peace and prosperity without the mental superiority of the powerful. This perception gives the powerful the legitimacy to control and tyrannize the powerless.

One consequence of this 'devolution' was the development of massive and pervasive centralization of authority and power, obviously in the hands of the few, whether they be warlords, monarchs, emperors, an aristocracy/patrician, or oligarchic class who make and enforce the rules. This process is aided and abetted by massive deskilling on a societal scale, reflected in the magical wishes for an omnipotent 'leader' who could address

---

[23] Edmund S. Morgan, <u>Inventing the People</u>, (New York, W.W. Norton, 1988), p. 306.

the fears and some of the helplessness of the people.[24] Fortunately, the emergence of more highly educated people gave ordinary people the opportunity to become a 'leader'. Without these highly educated people (engineers, technicians, professionals, etc.), these 'rulers' could not function and faced revolts and assassinations. The development of democratic methods of choosing leaders and the massive creation of material wealth through industrial capitalism facilitated this process enormously. In short, the many were becoming a threat to the few, with pushbacks most often ending in violent wars, revolutions, and counter-revolutions that humanity has had to experience in the last 250 years.

This process could be said to have reached its apogee in the 1970s, at least in the U.S., when the power elite commenced a backlash. The literary expression of this backlash was expressed in the Lewis Powell memorandum.. The memorandum served as a blueprint for the conservative backlash that began and called for the infiltration and remodelling of all aspects of American society. Both Ronald Reagan and Margaret Thatcher were its spokespersons and champions. They happily promoted neo liberal economic principles and TINA (there is no alternative) mantras as prescriptions necessary for the social, political, and economic retrenchment from the student rebellions, race riots, war protests, and other chaotic upheavals during the 1960s. It is also true that these responses of the 'power elites' could be seen as just another justification for their privileges, which rulers have done for centuries, by changing or revising the narrative.

What is happening at the 'leadership' level of Western elites is that there is another strata of hidden power and control that is not obvious to the vast majority of people. This strata is above the organizational, corporate, and financial elites that no one talks about, at least not through the mainstream media, or in the political and

----

[24] Gemmill, p. 113

academic arenas. It is this upper hidden level that is the real "rulers". So who are they? They are the billionaire class who own or control the majority of the world's wealth and the governments of the planet. In this class are some 200 families, highly concentrated in the powerful thirteen families that Fritz Springmeier and Robin de Ruiter have identified: Warburg, Russell, Rothschilds, Rockefellers, Du Pont, Onassis, Collins, Kennedy, Morgan, Hapsburg, Li, Bundy, and Astor[25]. For many decades, money and power in the world flowed to and from these families. One has to add the Royal family in England to the list as well as the many new billionaires that have emerged in the last three decades, including Bill Gates, Jeff Bezos, Elon Musk, and a number of high-tech billionaires. The current Covid pandemic crisis has greatly accelerated this concentration.

To be more precise, one is referring to a concentration of economic and political power in the hands of a self-serving elite who are fatal to democracy. As Charles Hugh Smith has put it, "When wealth buys concentrated political power, politics serves the interests of the super-wealthy and monopolies, not the citizenry…The extremely asymmetrical distribution of wealth in America is unprecedented. The recent essay *Monopoly Versus Democracy (Foreign Affairs, January 2021)* quantified this concentration of power:

> Nearly half of the new income generated since the global financial crisis of 2008 has gone to the wealthiest one percent of U.S. citizens. The richest three Americans collectively have more wealth than the poorest 160 million Americans.
> Other sources note that within this top 10%, wealth and income are highly concentrated in the top 0.1%. The next 4% (from 1% to 5%) own a smaller slice, and the following 5% (6% to 10%)

---

[25] Robin de Ruiter, Worldwide Evil and Misery: The Legacy of the 13 Satanic Bloodlines (Mayra Publications, 2014), p. 20.

own relatively little. In other words, the top 0.1% own virtually all the political power, as only they have the millions of dollars to buy political influence. The income of the top 1% households – currently around $500,000 – simply isn't enough to buy national political influence.

The bottom 90% own virtually no income-producing capital and are dependent on wages, which have been losing purchasing power for decades."[26]

There is another layer or more hidden layer, some believe, who are the real 'rulers' who stay behind the curtains behind the foregoing elites. One can only glimpse their presence at world meetings such as those held by the Bilderberger Conferences, the Council on Foreign Relations in the U.S., the Pilgrim Society, the Royal Institute of International Affairs, the Trilateral Commission, the Bank of International Settlements, the officers of the City of London, and the many secret societies that permeate American, British, French, and Italian societies. It is primarily through these secret, private, nonaccountable organizations that what one could call the Shadow people govern the planet and thereby rule the human race. Some refer to this group as the 'cabal'. The point here is that those people whom we think are our 'leaders' are anything but. They are just gofers and servants of this class of super wealthy and the psychopathic and sociopathic shadow rulers. And yet, the current dire and desperate state of the planet can be said to be due largely to the parasitic rulership of these people.

The question then becomes, how are these parasitic elites able to pull off such a magnitude of rulership and power over the 'many'? It is true that this 'takeover' was threatened by revolutions, wars, court battles, and political protests during the 18th, 19th, and 20th centuries that gave rise to more democratic forms of government and

---

[26] Charles Hugh Smith, Global Crisis, National Renewal (Oftwominds, 2021), p. 70.

egalitarian societies. The very notions of consent of the governed, the sovereignty of the people, majoritarian rule, inalienable human and civil rights, all challenged the values and thinking of the 'few' in the power elites for centuries. So, one has to ask, how have they survived? How have they maintained a state of affairs in which the few control the many?

According to historian Rutger Bregman, a change occurred in human history when humans evolved from hunter-gatherer nomadic lives to living in stable villages and communities. In the former, power distinctions between people were, if nomads tolerated them at all, temporary and served a purpose. Leaders were more knowledgeable, skilled, or charismatic. That is, they had the ability to get a given job done, which scientists refer to as achievement-based inequality. Nomadic peoples were allergic to inequality. Decisions were group affairs requiring long deliberation in which everybody got to have their say. People were universally concerned with being free from authority. It was taboo among hunter-gatherers to stockpile and hoard. People freely shared. This changed when humans built towns and villages. Populations grew, and life became more abundant. People now had belongings and land to fight over. Foraging nomads had a fairly laid-back membership policy. Villagers, on the other hand, grew more focused on their own communities and their own possessions. When humans began to band together with strangers, it was surprising to make war. Leaders emerged who proved their mettle on the battlefield. In time, these successful warlords grew so wedded to their authority that they no longer chose to give it up, even in peacetime. The successful generals or warlords made the leap to a permanent kingship. In short, the advent of settlements and private property had ushered in a new age in the history of humankind. The 1 per cent began oppressing the 99 per cent, and smooth talkers and manipulators ascended from commanders to generals, and from chieftains to kings. The days of liberty, equality, and fraternity were over.[27]

Bregman also points out that in ancient Athens, the cradle of Western democracy, two-thirds of the population were enslaved. Up until the French Revolution, almost all states everywhere were fueled by forced labour. Until 1800, at least three-quarters of the global population lived in bondage to a wealthy lord. More than 90% of the population worked the land, and more than 80% died in dire poverty. It has only been in the last two centuries that things have gotten better for the vast majority of people.[28]

From one perspective, the elites have been protected by the self-serving illusion that the state was permanent and could never fall. Protected by this illusion, the elites have devoted themselves to maximizing their own private gains, ignoring the consequences of their self-enrichment: a weakened economy, a corrupted polity, and an unravelling society, all of which generate fatal synergies.[29] The resilience of these elites is largely due to their ability to gradually and almost imperceptibly move from land-based warlords and aristocrats, with virtual control over the nation state, to financial and banking elites. The transformation of nations from agrarian societies to capitalist and from industrial capitalist to financial capitalist has accelerated this change. In short, plutocrats, bankers, lawyers, financial speculators, and fraudsters have taken over the commanding heights and management of the state. Their characteristics as amoral snakes belie their true and dangerous psychopathic natures.

To accomplish this takeover, or makeover, the ruling elites have also absorbed, compromised, and enlisted academics, the mass

---

[27] Rutger Bregman, Humankind: A hopeful history, (Little Brown, 2019), pp. 95-100.

[28] Ibid. pp. 108-111.

[29] Charles Hugh Smith, Global Crisis: National Renewal, p. 83.

media, and the bureaucratic regimes of the state. They have transformed the world economy into one run by cartels, monopolies, and giant oligopolies. For example, the concentration of power, control, and influence of 90% of the mass media in the U.S. can be attributed to five or six giant corporations, all of whom are controlled by billionaires and other large corporations (Viacom, AT&T, Comcast, Walt Disney Corp., News Corp, and Bloomberg media). Can anyone expect freedom of the press to survive in such an atmosphere?

Another example is the concentration of shareholder ownership. Three giant companies (BlackRock, Vanguard, and State Street) are the largest shareholders of 88% of the S&P 500 companies. Similar patterns of oligopolistic concentration can be seen in the automobile, oil and gas, banking, and pharmaceutical industries. If you are an unhappy shareholder, your power to bring a shareholder action against the giant companies is an illusion. You only have one remedy, and that is to sell your shares. If people have any stake in these corporations, it is through their pension funds, not as individual shareholders.

Overlying this economic structure are the central banks, privately owned by the financial elites, the world's wealthiest families. These banks, controlled in the West by the Bank of International Settlements (the central bankers' bank) in Basel, Switzerland, are the most powerful institutions on the planet. They are responsible for setting interest rates, currency valuations, and most importantly, the creation of money, which they do virtually out of thin air, and have a monopoly. They are currently planning on eliminating all cash currencies and replacing them with central bank digital currencies (CBDCs), which will allow banks to monitor each and every transaction a human does, automatically seize or freeze your money in your account, and tax or deduct what they want from your electronic money in your account. The plans are to introduce digital identity cards and passports that will record and rule your new '1984' life. Thus, the dominance of the global elites will be continued by and through an electronic prison camp, and humans will be reduced to neo-feudal dependence in debt-driven economies and global capital markets.

Rise of the Psychopaths

So far, this chapter has explained and discussed how the world has been controlled by the few, who are often referred to as the 'globalists'. Their management of economies and nation states via the banking system is just one of their tools of oppression and control. If there is 'leadership' amongst this elite, it can best be characterized as synthetic and artificial, inorganic and mechanistic. They seek to centralize power, a unipolar planet, exclusivity, unaccountable closed systems, and above all a complete lack of ethical awareness. They are composed of a high percentage of psychopaths and sociopaths who are seeking an end to humanity, though they will obviously never admit that. Humans will be replaced by transgender, technocratic, transhumanist cyborgs and AI robots on a massively depopulated planet. They assume humans are not capable of self-government and only they are fit to rule. That is why they are not really 'leaders'. They are rulers and everyone else is the ruled, whom they can control and exploit as serfs or digital plantation workers.

Obviously, if you are a member of the ruling class, one of your primary objectives is to maintain your rulership status. This task has grown increasingly complex and difficult to control in what some call the age of transparency via the internet, in which everything that the rulers do will be eventually exposed. The surveillance state technology is a two-way street that the rulers did not foresee. It is becoming increasingly difficult for them to hide behind the curtain, though mainstream or legacy media still strive to protect and shield them. The latter is a shadow of what they once were. Alternative news sites, independent journalists, and other information sources have proliferated. Hence, the increasing specter of government censorship of what can be seen on the internet with Google, Facebook, YouTube, etc. In spite of these countermeasures, people have come to see vast chunks of the media as fake news. One now sees fake personas, bots, fake scenarios (aka junk news), and quack experts known as pundits. At the end of the road, we are left with our "fake leaders," most recently seen in Joe Biden and Kamala Harris, though they are just a few of so many charlatans in powerful positions.

What this leads to is the confirmation of what Gemmell and Oakley referred to as the 'myth of leadership'. Our so-called leaders are mere puppets, dangling on the strings controlled by the 'rulers' above them, most often hidden. To maintain their control, the rulers have relied on reification, projection, and learned helplessness. As leadership author Warren Bennis has pointed out, this myth-making is an unconscious conspiracy, a social hoax, aimed at maintaining the status quo.[30] Reification is a social process which converts an abstraction or mental construct into a supposed reality.[31] Through reification, the social construction of leadership is mystified and accorded an objective reality, a false consciousness. According to Erich Fromm, the latter refers to the content of the conscious mind that is fictitious and has been introjected or assimilated without awareness through cultural programmes.[32]

Projection occurs when members of a group are faced with uncertainty and ambiguity regarding direction and often

---

[30] Gemmell and Oakley, p. 115.

[31] Ibid. p. 114.

[32] Ibid. p. 114.

experience feelings of anxiety, helplessness, discomfort, disappointment, hostility, and fear of failure. These emotions are ordinarily held in check by the prevailing social system and are dispelled by projecting them onto 'leadership' or the 'leader' role. The projection allows organizational members to avoid the conflicting and disturbing emotions and regress to a social order with which they are familiar.[33] In other words, they regress to their childhood, refuse to grow up, and expect "Mommy and Daddy' to rescue them. Such a social development is tailor-made for a tyrant or psychopath to exploit.

Social behaviour mimics this phenomena: massive learned helplessness, a social pathology characterized by an inability to imagine or perceive viable options along with accompanying feelings of despair and resistance to any form of action; religions that tell people all they have to do is believe and that a Messiah or magical leader will save them amplifies this; education institutions that fail to educate the young or provide them with the tools to become successful, self-sufficient and contributing adults, are a large part of the problem. Similarly, so are the many well-intentional socialist programmes that relieve one of his or her responsibility for their fate in life. An example is health care and the allopathic medical system promoted by 'big pharma.' All one has to do is go to a doctor and get some pills or surgery, and you will be cured. Very little attention or emphasis is placed on preventive care and natural cures such as eating natural products, not processed ones, proper rest and exercise, taking vitamin supplements, and taking time to care for your mental and psychological state. In short, our current medical system is built around three solutions: surgery, pills, and radiation, all three of which will kill people.

One ought to be curious how this sad state of affairs, which John Kenneth Galbraith referred to as a sociopathic, corporate plutocracy,

----

[33] Ibid. p. 114

came to be. If one understands this process, one can see how and why the many allow the few to rule them, and a sociopathic society to emerge. The term sociopathic is often used in conjunction with or in place of psychopathic. There is a lot of overlap in the psychological explanation of psychopaths, sociopaths, and malignant narcissists. The most distinguishing feature of a psychopath is their inability to feel empathy, compassion, and lack of a conscience. It is considered by many experts to be an incurable psychological malady. The 'gold standard' to test whether one is a psychopath has been the Psychopathy Checklist developed by Dr. Robert Hare. It lays out 22 items to assess human behaviour and includes the following:

1. Glibness/ superficial charm
2. Previous diagnosis as psychopath (or similar)
3. Egocentricity/ grandiose sense of self-worth
4. Proneness to boredom/ low frustration tolerance
5. Pathological lying and deception
6. Conning/ lack of sincerity
7. Lack of remorse or guilt
8. Lack of affect and emotional depth
9. Callous/ lack of empathy
10. Parasitic lifestyle
11. Short-tempered/ poor behavioural controls
12. Promiscuous sexual relations
13. Early behaviour problems
14. Lack of realistic, long-term plans
15. Impulsivity
16. Irresponsible behaviour as a parent
17. Frequent marital relations
18. Juvenile delinquency
19. Poor probation or parole risk
20. Failure to accept responsibility for own actions
21. Many types of offense

22. Drug or alcohol abuse is not the direct cause of antisocial behaviour.

Other characteristics include double-mindedness, invented personas, shallow emotions, power seeking, invoking pity, and a morally debauched lifestyle. In short, a psychopath is a person who lacks a conscience, feels no remorse or guilt or empathy, and can do a remarkable job of hiding these characteristics. What is shocking is to apply this list to so many of our 'rulers' and 'leaders' in almost every field and see what is staring you in the face. Hare, at one point, claimed psychopaths comprised one to two percent of the general population. However, among the ruling classes, high-functioning psychopaths number many multiples of that.

A sociopath shares many of the above characteristics. A sociopath is defined by the Diagnostic and Statistical Manual of Mental Disorders (DSM) as a psychiatric classification of what is considered as an anti-social behaviour, a pervasive pattern of disregard for and violation of the rights of others. It consists of a failure to conform to social norms with respect to lawful behaviour (as indicated by repeatedly performing acts that are grounds for arrest), deception (repeatedly lying, use of aliases, conning others), impulsiveness, irritability and aggressiveness, reckless disregard for the safety of others, indifferent to or rationalizing having hurt, mistreated or stolen from another).[34] According to Paul Babiak and Robert Hare in their book "Snakes into Suits", sociopathy also more commonly refers to compositions or arrays of attitudes and behaviors that society considers criminal or antisocial, but are considered acceptable, normal, even necessary for a particular subculture or specific social environment. Common examples include the mafia, street gangs, secret societies and drug cartels. One distinction of a sociopath from a psychopath is that the former's overt criminal

---

[34] Charles Derber, Sociopathic Society: A peoples sociology of the United States (Boulder Colorado, Paradigm Publishers), 2013, p. 10.

behaviour makes them much easier to identify. A sociopath is much more likely to end up behind bars than a psychopath. Psychopaths are much harder to spot, and if they are high functioning and highly intelligent, there is almost no limit to the heights to which they may rise in an organization. An example of this can be seen in a man like Heinrich Himmler in Nazi Germany. He was one of the senior Nazis and used his SS Gestapo soldiers to commit unspeakable crimes. But his loyal followers and henchmen in the SS were more often sociopaths or psychopath enablers. Texe Marrs refers to these people as 'protopsychopaths', often being the associates or partners of the psychopaths. A protopsychopath is someone who has attached themselves to a *spellbinding* psychopath. They are useful to the psychopath by obediently carrying out various wicked deeds. They are not usually full psychopaths. Marrs also refers to psychopaths as 'soul eaters'. Jungian psychiatrist James Hollis, looking closely at the etymology of the word, refers to psychopathology as literally the suffering of the soul.[35] Some would even go so far as to say that lacking a conscience and being incapable of feeling empathy means you have no soul.

What has to baffle an ordinary, sane, or ethical person is how people with such traits can become so powerful. When humans lived more nomadic, hunter-gatherer human communities were much smaller, often not exceeding 150 people. Leadership was temporary, and decisions were made as a group. Anyone who was too boastful, selfish, and greedy was much more easily identifiable and would face expulsion from the tribe and likely face starvation. With the advent of the first settlements and the growth in equality, the chieftains and kings had to start legitimising why they enjoyed more privileges than their subjects. Consequently, they began engaging in

---

[35] James Hollis, A Life of Meaning; Relocating your center of spiritual gravity (Boulder Colorado, Sounds True), 2023, p. 12.

propaganda. The modest chief of the nomadic tribe was replaced by a King who proclaimed he ruled by divine right or that he was himself a god. Today, we have designed ingenious ideologies to justify why some individuals 'deserve' more authority, status, and wealth than others. In capitalist societies, we tend to use the argument of *merit*. But how do you decide who has the most merit? Solders, bankers, lawyers, or garbage bin men? A disruptor is anyone who is thinking outside the box. But the better you spin yourself, the bigger your piece of the pie. In fact, you could look at the entire evolution of civilization as a history of rulers who continually devised new justifications for their privileges.[36]

One such useful "myth" is 'God'. One does not have to be an atheist to question the belief in an omnipotent God. Or a god angered by human sin. Some scientists have come up with a fascinating theory related to the unique aspect of human eyes. Thanks to the whites surrounding our irises, we can follow the direction each other's gazes and one can get a glimpse into other people's minds, which is vital to forge bonds of trust. Once humans began living together in large groups alongside thousands of strangers, everything changed. We literally lost sight of each other. There is no way one can make eye contact with thousands or tens of thousands or a million people, so our mutual distrust began to grow. Eventually, people started to suspect that others were sponging off the community, while everyone else was breaking their backs. So, the 'rulers' had to figure out a way to keep tabs on the masses, someone who heard and saw everything. This role was given to God, an all-seeing Eye. And who presided over its role, the priesthood. It was no accident that the new deities were vengeful.[37] Today, as the role of churches and God has diminished compared to centuries ago, the

---

[36] Rutger Bregman, <u>Humankind: A Hopeful History</u>, pp. 231-232.
[37] Ibid. pp.353-354.

elites have created a new 'god', that being high tech, and constant surveillance.

What undoubtedly accelerated this evolution, which could also be described as a devolution, is the emergence of armies and their commanders. One would be very foolish to try and stand up to a strongman who has all opposition skinned, burned alive, or drawn and quartered. One's criticism then won't seem so urgent. So, from this point on, gods and kings were not so easily ousted, and not backing the 'myth' could now prove fatal.[38]

While this may seem obvious to us in the 21st century, what is not so obvious is that so many of our social, economic, and political institutions are tailor-made for these myth-based rulers to take control. In the words of Yuval Noah Harari, "complex human societies seem to require imagined hierarchies and unjust discrimination."[39] Perversely, once these 'rulers' take control, they are exceedingly difficult to remove. Humans have unconsciously created 'dominator cultures' to justify this. A dominator culture is driven by a death wish, an urge to control, an urge to violate, and an urge to destroy life, and is motivated primarily by power and profit. Examples include the massive killing of 60 to 80 million people in the First and Second World Wars in the 20th century, the genocide and massacre of the native Americans, the holocaust, the genocide of the Ukrainian people, the deaths of 500,000 children in Iraq, and many other unspeakable crimes against humanity in the last several centuries. One could also include the massive pollution our industrial economy creates and the extinction and destruction of practically all animal and plant life in one form or another.

----

[38] Ibid. p. 236.
[39] Ibid. p. 237.

Now, it is probably unfair to single out Western civilization as the culprit, as it is one of many dominant cultures to have existed in the last 10,000 years. Practically every human civilization that has ever existed has generated such a culture; the ancient Greeks and Romans, the Chinese, Mongolian, Persian, Mayan, and Aztec, and others. In the last two thousand years, one could count on one hand the number of decades in which men were not at war somewhere on the planet. So, one can ask, if there were no such human beings as psychopaths or sociopaths, would the same events have taken place? The answer suggested here is probably not.

Wetiko

To test this hypothesis, one can look to the indigenous culture that Columbus encountered when he reached the West Indies. What he found there were native people, generous, kind, loving, living so radically different from the way of life of Europeans. He reported,

> ...since they have become more assured, and are losing that terror, they are artless and generous, to such a degree as no one would believe but him who had seen it. Of anything they have, if it be asked for, they never say no, but rather invite the person to accept it, and show as much lovingness as though they would give their hearts...And they know no sect nor idolatry, save that they all believe that power and goodness are in the sky...And this comes not because they are ignorant; on the contrary, they are men of very subtle wit, who navigate all those seas, and who give a marvelous good account of everything...And as soon as I arrived in the Indies, in the first island that I found, I took some of them by force...[40]

In actuality, Columbus and the Spaniards took thousands of these natives and sold them into slavery. The West Indies were

---

[40] Jack D. Forbes, <u>Columbus and Other Cannibals</u> (New York, Seven Stories Press, 2008), p. 21.

depopulated of native peoples. It was the first of many such acts of genocide by European settlers.

What is most revealing of these incidents is how the natives saw this invasion. As history and most explanations of past events are written by the victors, the indigenous peoples' perceptions of what was happening to them have rarely been told or taught to non-natives. One reason is that the truth and real reasons for the genocide are too threatening to the European self-identity and raison d'être. Can you admit very happily that all the land you occupy was stolen? Yet, the indigenous perception of what was happening is crucial to our understanding of what is destroying life on this planet today. What the natives saw was not an advanced civilization overtaking them but a diseased and plague-ridden civilization that would destroy everything in its path to claim ownership. This plague is known by native North Americans as 'wetiko', a malignant egophrenia. It is a psychospiritual pathology of the soul. While ontologically real, it is a non-local psychic virus existing outside a dimension of time, and living in a world whose coordinates cannot be plotted in astronomical space or time or situated on a map. The best that we can do is to find local traces of its nonlocal, multidimensional field of operations. According to Paul Levy, who has studied the wetiko phenomena, the 'wetiko/malignant egophrenia exists in a place that is not in the geography of our three-dimensional world. Unlike a physical virus, the wetiko/malignant egophrenia cannot be isolated materially, but its characteristic signature can be detected and seen in the peculiar operations of a psyche that is under its spell.[41]

---

[41] Paul Levy, Dispelling Wetiko: Breaking the Curse of Evil (Berkeley, California, North Atlantic Books), 2013, pp. 5-6.

The question one has to ask now is how is that we know or can know that this 'wetiko' energy exists? Were the native North Americans delusional, or were they on to something? To answer these questions, one has to ask what does the term 'wetiko' means or refers to. It is best to think of it as a psychic blindness, daemonic energy, collective psychosis, or psychological disease that is not recognized by Western medical professions as such. Writers like Paul Levy, author of <u>Dispelling Wetiko: Breaking the Curse of Evil</u>, and <u>Wetiko: Healing the Mind Virus That Plagues Our World</u>, and Jack D. Forbes, author of <u>Columbus and Other Cannibals</u>, have written deeply about it. The indigenous people have been tracking this 'psychic mind virus' for centuries, calling it 'wetiko' in Cree, windigo in Ojibwa, or wintiko in Powhatan. For them it is a psycho-spiritual disease and refers to a diabolically wicked person or spirit who terrorizes others by means of evil acts. It is a psychosis in the true sense of the word, and moreover, a sickness of the soul or spirit, an archetypical psycho-spiritual pathology of the soul. If you do not or cannot see or imagine a human soul, you will never see it. And those who cannot see beyond the confines of empirical, scientific materialism usually have the most difficulty. According to Levy is the best we can do is find traces of its nonlocal multidimensional field of operations.[42] Yet these 'traces' are all around and within us:

> Wetiko is a cannibalizing force driven by insatiable greed, appetite without satisfaction, consumption as an end in itself, and war for its own sake, against other tribes, species, and nature, even against the individual's own humanity. It is a disease of the soul, and being a disease of the soul, we all potentially have wetiko, as it pervades and "in-forms" the underlying field of consciousness. Any one of us at any moment can fall into our unconsciousness and unwittingly become an instrument for the evil of wetiko to act itself out through us and incarnate in our world. If we see someone who seems to be taken over by wetiko and we think they have the

---

[42] Ibid. p. 5.

disease and we don't, in seeing them as separate, we have fallen under the spell of the virus ourselves.

Wetiko induces in us a proclivity to see the source of our own pathology outside of ourselves – existing in the other. Wetiko feeds off of polarization and fear – and terror—of the other.[43]

In short, it is a form of parasite that feeds off the negative emotions of fear, anxiety, regret, resentment, and depression. Conversely, it is defeated by human emotions such as joy, happiness, compassion, caring, satisfaction, and most of all, love. Its cure, then, potentially lies within us.[44] But our failure to recognize it only makes it more powerful. As Levy has put it, the wetiko epidemic is the manifestation of something in our shared collective conscious taking on a material form and demands our attention:

> Wetiko is literally demanding that we pay attention to the fundamental role that the psyche (the source of our dreams) plays in creating our experience of ourselves and of the world. Forgetting the crucial role that the psyche plays in creating our experience, we marginalize our own intrinsic authority, tragically dreaming up both internal and external authoritarian forces to limit our freedom and mold our experience for us. Never before in all [recorded] human history has our species been forced to confront the numinous, world-transforming powers of the psyche on so vast a scale.[45]

When displayed or seen in the individual human, wetiko very closely resembles psychopathy. All the traits that psychopaths express are also expressions of wetiko. Full-blown

---

[43] Paul Levy, Wetiko: Healing the Mind-Virus That Plagues our World, (Rochester, Vermont, Inner Traditions), 2021, p. 9.
[44] Ibid. p. 12.
[45] Ibid. pp. 14-15.

wetikos or Big Wetikos are not in touch with their own humanity and therefore cannot see the humanity in others. This is reflected in the psychopathic traits as a lack of empathy and compassion, amongst others. Both Levy and Forbes agree that wetiko is now a massive psychic epidemic. Like a fractal, wetiko operates on multiple dimensions simultaneously – intra-personally (within individuals) and interpersonally (among ourselves), and collectively (as a species), as well as trans-personally (in a realm beyond our personal selves). Those afflicted with wetiko consume, like a cannibal, the life force of others – human and nonhuman – for private purpose or profit, and do so without giving back something of their own lives.[46] Levy further defines wetiko as a 'cannibal sickness'; symbolically speaking, cannibalism has to do with feasting on another's soul, or in our case, the soul of humanity. Thus, the point of attack for the struggle against the evil of wetiko is the human soul.[47]

Forbes believed that this psychic epidemic can be traced to the arrival of the Europeans to the Americas. He notes that for thousands of years human beings have suffered from a plague, worse than leprosy, a sickness worse than malaria, and a malady more terrible than smallpox. It is 'cult of 'aggression and violence' that reigns supreme, and has produced a 'dominating' culture that is excruciatingly, relentlessly, insanely, genocidally, ecocidally, and suicidally destructive. It is the disease of aggression against other living things, and more precisely, the disease of the consuming of other creatures' lives and possessions. Imperialism, colonialism, torture, enslavement, conquest, brutality, lying, cheating, secret police, greed, rape, terrorism are only words until we are touched by them and our lives are changed forever. In Forbes' words, this is the greatest epidemic sickness known to man.[48]

---

[46] Levy, Dispelling Wetiko, p. 13.
[47] Levy, Wetiko: Healing the Mind Virus That Plagues our World, p. 35.

[48] Forbes, p. xvi..

One should ask how modern Western civilization has not noticed this disease? Certainly, Sigmund Freud in his work Civilization and Its Discontents, and Carl Jung have written about it, as well as many other social scientists. Recently, Mattias Desmet, a psychologist and statistician from Belgium, has come forth in his work The Psychology of Totalitarianism and described a very similar phenomena, which he calls "mass formation psychosis" (MFP), a form of mass hypnosis or madness of crowds. It affects 20-30% of the population. According to Dr. Robert W. Malone, the conditions to set up mass formation psychosis include a lack of social connectedness and sense making, as well as large amounts of latent anxiety and passive aggression. When people are inundated with a narrative that presents a plausible "object of anxiety" and a strategy for coping with it, then many individual groups will possibly band together to battle the object with a collective single-mindedness. This allows people to stop focusing on their own problems and avoid personal mental anguish by focusing all their energy on the new object. As this crowd psychosis grows, the group becomes increasingly bonded and connected. They become unable to consider alternative points of view, and their leaders become revered, incapable of any wrong. This is not group think, but something more pernicious. Group think can fall apart, but mass formation psychosis is different. A hypnotized crowd cannot so easily break free of the narrative. Examples include Nazi Germany in the 1930s and 1940s, and the recent Covid 19 pandemic hysteria. In each case, the solution for those in control is to tell bigger lies to prop up the solutions proposed.[49]

There are several notable differences between 'wetiko' and mass formation psychosis (MFP). The latter is almost

---

[49] Dr. Robert Malone; https://rwmalonemd.substack.com/p/mass-formation-psychosis?

exclusively a mass occurrence. Wetiko could refer to one person in the tribe infected with the wetiko 'virus'. Or it could refer to a whole tribe or nation so infected, as Jack Forbes does in referring to Columbus and the Spanish Conquistadors. Secondly, the wetiko 'virus' is one that affects people at a very deep psychological and spiritual level. The perfect carrier of this mind virus is a psychopath, and as many experts believe, psychopaths are incurable. A society afflicted with MFP can be cured, according to Desmet, if enough of the population realized and woke up to the lies they have been fed. This understandably takes time, and much communication, even relearning. Thirdly, the wetiko 'virus' implies and contains a violation of ethical and natural law by those infected. It can be seen and felt by tribal shamans and elders and identified as evil. MFP, however, most often occurs in situations in which it is much more difficult to ascribe blame or guilt to the perpetrators in our modern, technologically dependent societies. The power of the mass media is ubiquitous and penetrating via the internet, television, newspapers, magazines, and now social media. It is therefore a force that can deliver humanity to a 1984 dystopia if people are not thinking intelligently and critically, and listening. The horrifying, cynical, and dehumanizing words of Yuval Harari, Klaus Schwab's favorite futurist, express this:

> Again, I think the biggest question in maybe economics and politics of the coming decades will be what to do with all these useless people?[50]

> The problem is more boredom and what to do with them, and how they will find some sense of meaning in life, when they are basically meaningless and worthless.

> My best guess, at present, is a combination of drugs and computer games as a solution for [most]. It is already happening. Under

---

[50] Forbidden Knowledge TV transcript.

different titles, different headings, you see more and more people spending more and more time solving inner problems with drugs and computer games, both legal and illegal drugs...

I think once you are superfluous, you don't have power...I don't think that the masses, even if they somehow organize themselves, stand much of a chance. We are not Russia of 1917 or in the 19th century...

But think about the world, say in 50 years, 100 years, where the poor people continue to die, but the rich people, in addition to all the other things they get, also get an exemption from death. Once you really solve a problem like direct brain-computer interface, when brains and computers can interact directly; for example -- to take just one example – that's it, that's the end of history; that's the end of biology, as we know it....[51]

Could Joseph Goebbels, Hitler's propaganda minister, have expressed an MFP any better?

Our Oligarchic Societies

One could spend days dissecting, decoding, and deconstructing Harari's dystopian, Orwellian, technocratic diatribe against everything human. Yet, his views represent the official narrative that governments, corporations, especially Big Tech, have consciously and surreptitiously subjected humanity via indoctrination. They also reflect the thinking and values of many of the elites and upper classes who have ruled humanity.

The upper classes of human societies are almost immune today to the risks of change in the status quo that does not favor them. Without this protection, they would risk losing their power, status, and wealth. The working classes know from

---

[51] From a speech of Hariri on Forbidden Knowledge's web site

difficult and hard, deprived life experiences that those above them have repressed and exploited their labor from time immemorial. It is from the middle classes, which have emerged and grown in size enormously since 1789 in the West, that more people have begun to awaken, largely due to their increased wealth, education, and labor rights protection, and most recently in the last several decades from the information explosion and transparency of the internet. The latter has caused a social and economic revolution comparable to the Gutenberg Press during the Renaissance.

So why do the elites lie to their fellow humans? One reason just stated is to protect their privileged status. But there are other reasons. Another is their Malthusian, zero-sum, fixed pie thinking, the belief that if someone else gains, I lose. Another is to hide the level of corruption and incompetence in their ranks. One of the most compelling reasons, however, is the level of corruption, incompetence, and evil in their ranks. James Burnham, in his classic work, The Machiavellians: Defenders of Freedom, has pointed to the failure of our scientific elites to deal with the dilemmas and obstacles for political action. He argued that it is exceedingly difficult for men and women to be scientific or logical about social and political problems. The elites have the advantage over the masses of people through the possession of more knowledge, more free time from the burden of getting food and shelter, and no doubt certain talents given their privileged education and social and economic positions. But they are also subject to the inescapable corruptions of power and privilege. As Burnham points out, those who have privileges almost always develop false or distorted ideas about themselves. Moreover, they are under a compulsion to deceive themselves and others through some kind of irrational theory which seeks to justify their monopoly of those privileges, rather than explain away the annoying and self-deprecating truths about how those privileges were acquired and are held.[52]

Burnham also contends the life of the masses and the cohesion of society demand the acceptance of myths. A scientific attitude towards society does not permit the acceptance of myths; "But the leaders must profess, indeed foster, a belief in myths, or the fabric of society will crack and they will be overthrown. In short, the leaders, if they themselves are scientific, must lie. It is hard to lie all the time in public, but to keep privately an objective regard for the truth. Not only is it hard; it is often ineffective, for lies are often not convincing when told with a divided heart. The tendency is for the deceivers to become self-deceived, to believe their own myths."[53] They think they have escaped Plato's Cave and have seen the light, but are still trapped by the shadows in it, blinded by their illusions. This explains why practically all politicians are surrounded by public relations experts and media 'presstitutes' as Paul Craig Roberts refers to them.

Mass psychologist Mattias Desmet echoes Burnham's observations. He has expressed the view that fully fledged totalitarianism requires a diabolical pact between the elites and the masses. To accomplish this, the elites use propaganda excessively and relentlessly. They have wedded themselves to the rationalism and materialism of the Enlightenment, which replaced the ethical and religionist view of man in the world. But the rational essence of life can never be the ultimate guiding light of a society. It will eventually, as Huval Harrari's language reveals, lapse into radical irrationalism. It will in the end lead to a society in which people lose all ethical awareness, and this can be seen in every totalitarian system that has emerged, including

---

[52] James Burnham, The Machiavellians: Defenders of Freedom, (Borough, Lume Books) 1943, p. 243.
[53] Ibid. pp. 243-244.

fascism, communism, or modern technocratic transhumanism. Ironically, and tragically, the elites controlling the totalitarian system deliberately choose this as it works to preserve their rulership.[54]

What the foregoing discussion does not reveal is that there are two very distinct and recognizable forms of rulership, which many call leadership, that are possible expressions in the great awakening of the 21st century. So far, the discussion has referred directly or obliquely to what could be more accurately described as inorganic, artificial, synthetic, or fake 'leadership' stemming from domineering, restrictive, and parasitic cultures. This could be contrasted with "organic' leadership, which is more natural, balanced, inclusive, and life-affirming. It relies upon a balanced left and right brain hemisphere. The violent and destructive fruits of this former kind of rulership are plain to see everywhere: pogroms, witch hunts, wars, religious crusades, slave labour, gulags, genocide, ecocide, death squads, satanic child abuse, and many other vile, cruel, and evil human behaviours. Has anything been left out from this list? The history of humanity is a virtual catalogue of these monstrous criminal acts. Yet, as it says in the Bible, and useful to remember, by their fruits ye shall know them.

Another fundamental attribute of this kind of rulership is the rule of the many by the few. Perhaps the many truly but, naively, believe the few will save them from these vile and horrible human outcomes or that their numbers will save them. Unfortunately, the few view them as expendable farm animals, useless eaters, chattels, and cannon fodder in their wars of aggression and expansion. The Georgia Guidestones was a monument to their perverted and mendacious hopes and values.

---

[54] From Mattias Desmet's comments at U.S. Senate hearings, presided over by Senator Ron Johnson in 2024 dealing with "Federal Health Agencies and the covid cartel. What are they hiding?"

The oligarchic nature of so many so-called "democratic" societies is also proof of this fake leadership. The myth is that democracy means government of the people, by the people, and for the people, and that those who govern govern with the consent of the people. But where is the evidence of this form of government in reality? Looking back at the last several thousand years of recorded history, one can see oligarchic systems triumphant everywhere. As Murray Rothbard has pointed out in his book Conceived in Liberty, even the United States, from the moment of its Constitutional conception, was an oligarchic creature in form and substance.

Another prominent feature of these "rulers" is their bias and outspoken preference for centralization and control as opposed to decentralization, laissez-faire, and the maximization of human freedom. And accompanying centralization are its accoutrements: mechanization, or the mechanical view of life, technocracy, transhumanism, and scientific materialism. This characteristic became increasingly obvious as the 20th century unfolded, and has reached a new crescendo in the 21st century, as governments pass more laws and impose more taxes and restrictions on people. Internationally, it can be seen in the pervasive and ubiquitous growth of international institutions connected to the U.N., like UNESCO, and other bodies like the World Health Organization and the World Economic Forum. The obvious advantage of this development is that it empowers the few thousand families at the top, who own more wealth than the rest of humanity, to control the many, now over eight billion people. And when the few are comprised and led by psychopathic and sociopathic individuals, it becomes easy to foresee a dystopian totalitarian form of society most likely to emerge.

The third characteristic giving rise to 'rulership', as opposed to an organic, non-elitist approach, is how the 'rulers' perceive humans. As mentioned, many of these rulers see humans as inorganic, artificial, non-conscious, non-sovereign objects or 'things'. They therefore can be cloned, enslaved, treated as cattle, to be chipped, euthanized, slaughtered, and subject to any form of malevolent, even sinister treatment that they deem necessary. Their views mirror the European settlers' perceptions of the indigenous people of North America as soulless savages, with whom they could do whatever they wanted. After all, if you didn't have a soul, you were not a human. At the end of the day, these 'sub-humans' become just another form of 'property' to them. Human slavery may have been legally abolished, but has re-emerged as modern global neo-feudalism through usury, causing debt slavery, human trafficking, child labour, drug addiction, and much more. Their goal is to create a new or post 'human.' A post-human or human 2.0 is someone who has been modified with performance-enhancing drugs and mechanical and computer chip implants to the point where a person is no longer human but is really a silicon cyborg.[55] The descriptive phrase used to describe this development is 'transhumanism'. Even Hollywood has joined the chorus with movies like AI, Artificial Intelligence, Surrogates, I Robot, The Matrix, Minority Report, and many others. Silicon entrepreneurs have already forecasted the obsolescence of smartphones, which will be replaced by implants in the human brain. They claim their technologies will enable the blind to see and the paralyzed to walk. What they are not saying is that these new technologies will enable governments, intelligence agencies, and corporations to monitor, watch, tax, and control humanity 24/7 with a high-tech panopticon surveillance system with greater efficiency than any other authoritarian, totalitarian regime in human history. It will be an age of digital feudalism. Anyone familiar with the thoughts of Ray Kurweil or has read Orwell's 1984, Huxley's Brave New World knows what this will mean for humanity. Or you could listen to any speech in the last few years by

---

[55] Daniel Estulin, TransEvolution: The Coming Age of Human Deconstruction (Chicago, Independent Publishers Group) 2014, p.172.

WEF's in-house 'philosopher' Yuval Noah Harari if you don't care to read his writing such as <u>Homo Deus; A Brief History of Tomorrow</u>.

One could spend days dissecting, decodifying, and deconstructing Harari's dystopian, Orwellian, technocratic diatribe against everything human. Yet, his views represent the official narrative that governments, corporations, especially Big Tech, have consciously and surreptitiously subjected humanity via indoctrination. To resist this entrainment requires making an effort to proactively seek out and expose oneself to information and perspectives that challenge the ideas and values expressed by these entities. Only then can one gain a more objective, balanced, and credible understanding of the world. At this stage, a more rewarding exercise will be to replace our current 'elite rulers' with people who will prevent this dark scenario from ever happening. If it happens, future historians might refer to it as the "Great Purge."

REFERENCES

Babiak Paul, and Hare, Robert D. Snakes in Suits: Understanding and Surviving the Psychopaths in Your Office. New York: Harper Business, (2007).

Boddy, Clive R. Corporate Psychopaths: Organizational Destroyer. United Kingdom: Pelgrave Macmillan, 2011.

Boddy, Clive R., Richard K. Ladyshewsky, and Peter Galvin. "The Influence of Corporate Psychopaths on Corporate Social Responsibility and Organizational Commitment to Employees." Journal of Business Ethics (2010) 97:1-19.

Bregman, Rutger. Humankind: A Hopeful History. New York: Little, Brown and Company, 2019.

Burnham, James. The Machiavellians. Borough, U.K.: Lume Books, 1943.

Cleckey, Hervey. The Mask of Sanity. Augusta, GA: Emily Cleckey, (1980).

Derber, Charles. Sociopathic Society. Boulder, Colorado: Paradigm Publishers, 2013.

Desmet, Mattias. The Psychology of Totalitarianism. White River Junction, Vermont: Chelsea Green Publishing, 2022.

Estulin, Daniel. TransEvolution: The Coming Age of Human Deconstruction. Walterville, OR: Trine Day, 2014.

Forbes, Jack D. Columbus and Other Cannibals. New York: Seven Stories Press,1979.

Gemmill, Gary, and Judith Oakley. "Leadership: An Alienating Social Myth?" Human Relations 45 (2) (1992): 113-129.

Gill, Roger. Theory and Practice of Leadership (Second Edition). London: Sage Publications, 2011.

Harari, Yuval Noah. Homo Deus: A Brief History of Tomorrow. New York: HarperCollins, 2017.

Hare, Robert D. Without Conscience: The Disturbing World of the Psychopaths Among Us. New York: Guilford Press, 1993.

Harrington, Alan. Psychopaths... NewYork, Simon and Schuster, 1972.

Hodson, Gordon, and Sarah Hogg, and Cara C. MacInnis. "The role of "dark personalities" (narcissism, Machiavellianism, psychopathy): Big Five personality factors, and ideology in explaining prejudice." Journal of Research in Personality 43 (2009) 686-690.

James Hollis. A Life of Meaning: Relocating Your Center of Spiritual Gravity. Boulder, Colorado: Sounds True, 2023.

Lobaczewski, Andrew M. Political Ponerology: A Science on the Nature of Evil Adjusted for Political Progress, Toronto: Red Pill Press (2006).

Lash, John Lamb. Not in His Image. White River Junction, Vermont: Chelsea Green Publishing, 2012.

Levy, Paul. Dispelling Wetiko: Breaking the Curse of Evil. Berkeley, CA: North Atlantic Books, 2013.

Levy, Paul. Wetiko: Healing the Mind-Virus That Plagues our World. Rochester, Vermont: +4110 Inner Traditions, 2021.

Macoby, Michael. "Narcissistic Leaders: The Incredible Pros, the Inevitable Cons." Harv 36ard Business Review January-February 2000, 69-77.

Machiavelli, Niccolo. Trans. Hill Thompson. The Prince. (1513). Norwalk, Conn. The Easton Press, 1980.

Morgan, Edmund S. Inventing the People. New York: W.W. Norton, 1988.

Nielsen, Jeffrey S. The Myth of Leadership: Creating Leaderless Organizations. Palo Alto, California: Davies-Black Publishing, 2004.

Padilla, Art, Robert Hogan, and Robert Kaiser. "The toxic triangle: Destructive leaders, susceptible followers and conducive environments." The Leadership Quarterly 18 (2007) 176-194.

Paulhus, Delroy L. and Kevin M. Williams. "The Dark Triad of personality: Narcissism, Machiavellianism, and psychopathy." Journal of Research in Personality 36 (2002) 556-563.

Petrides, K.V., Philip A. Vernon, Julie Aitkin Schermer, and Livia Veselka. "Trait Emotional Intelligence and the Dark Triads of Personality." Twin Research and Human Genetics 14 (No.1) (2011) 35-41.

Rosenthal, Seth A. and Todd L. Pittinsky. "Narcissistic Leadership." The Leadership Quarterly 17 (2006) 617-633.

Ruiter, Robin de. Worldwide Evil and Misery: The Legacy of the 13 Satanic Bloodlines. The Netherlands, Mayra Publications, 2008.

Sheridan, Thomas. Defeated Demons: Freedom from Consciousness Parasites in Psychopathic Society. Velluminous Press, 2012.

Smith, Charles Hugh. Global Crisis, National Renewal: A (Revolutionary) Grand Strategy for the United States. Hilo, HI: Oftwominds, 2021.

Smith, Charles Hugh. Inequality and the Collapse of Privilege. Berkeley, California: Oftwominds, 2016.

Smith, Charles Hugh. Money & Work Unchained. Berkeley, California: Oftwominds, 2017.

Springmeier, Fritz. Bloodlines of the Illuminati, Volume 1. iLLamanti Research Group 2019.

Springmeier, Fritz. Bloodlines of the Illuminati, Volume 2. iLLamanti Research Group, 2019.

Stout, Martha. The Sociopath Next Door. New York: Harmony, (2006).

Valeri, Don. The Origins of Servant Leadership: Servant Leadership's Past and Potential Future. Saarbrucken, Germany: Lambert Academic Publishing, 2007.

Xenophon, Translation by Walter Miller. Cyropaedia. Cambridge, Mass.: Harvard University Press, 1914.

Xenophon, Translation by Carleton L. Brownson. Anabasis. Cambridge, Mass.: Harvard University Press, 1922.

Chapter Three

The Leader's Shadow: Friend Or Foe?

Luke: Is the dark side stronger?
Yoda: No, no...but easier, more seductive.
Luke: But how will I know the good side from the bad?
Yoda: You will know when you are calm, at peace, passive...A Jedi uses the force for knowledge and defence, never attacks.
Luke: But tell me why?
Yoda: No, no...there is no why...Nothing more will I teach you today. Clear your mind of questions.
Luke: There is something not right. I feel cold.
Yoda: That place is strong, the dark side of the force, a remain of evil it is. In it you must go.
Luke: What's in there?
Yoda: Only what you take with you. Your weapons, you will not need them.

Lawrence Kasdan, from the motion picture The Empire Strikes Back

Most of our modern leadership literature deals with the various types of leadership. Definitions and theories proliferate and pour forth onto the internet, our bookstores, and libraries. Little of it, unfortunately, deals intimately or extensively with the dark side of leadership. Those who have, like Barbara Kellerman, Jean Lipman-Blumen, M.F.R., Kets de Vries, and Parker Palmer, tell us that this is due to our obsession with defining "good" leadership. Fewer still tell us anything profound or incisive of this mostly unconscious dark force that sooner or later afflicts all leaders. We seem to have operated on the naïve assumption that finding good leaders will not require us to weed out those who have failed to deal with their shadows. The time has come to take a closer look at why this happens, what leaders are confronted with by it, and how they can deal their own illusive dark side.

There are at least two significant reasons for this. One reason, as Barbara Kellerman has pointed out, is the need to encourage the probability of good leadership by getting as many people as possible to explore bad leadership. How can we realistically ever grapple with that which we do not understand?[1] The second is to raise the consciousness of our leaders by making sure they have grown enough inside to lead on the outside. It is submitted that this is not merely a psychological journey but a spiritual one as well.

Background:

As James MacGregor Burns put it in 1978, "the key to understanding leadership lies in recent findings and concepts in psychology."[2] Given the social upheaval of the 1970s, when Burns wrote his book <u>Leadership</u>, it is understandable why he was attracted to the humanistic thinking of the psychologist Abraham Maslow. In the wake of the Vietnam War and Watergate, reading Maslow was like a breath of fresh air. But one needs to go further back when considering the "dark side" from a psychological perspective, and look at the contributions of two of psychology's greatest minds, Sigmund Freud and Carl Jung.

Freud's concepts dealing with the primal father, transference, and narcissism have been major contributions to the study of

----

[1] Barbara Kellerman, <u>Bad Leadership: What it is, How it Happens, Why it Matters.</u> (Boston: Harvard Business School Press, 2004). Pp. 12-13.

[2] James MacGregor Burns, <u>Leadership.</u> (New York: Harper & Row, 1978). p. 49.

dysfunctional leadership.[3] In <u>Psychopathology of Everyday Life</u> (1901), Freud examined the hidden agendas that undermine consciousness and produce the apparent mistakes (Freudian slips) that were symbolic manifestations of another darker will flowing beneath the surface of the conscious mind.[4] Years later, Freud wrote his <u>Civilization and Its Discontents</u> (1927-1931), in which he cast the unconscious as a boiling cauldron of evil, violent, and destructive impulses. The raison d'être of civilization was to guard and control these impulses before they overwhelmed everyone and everything and exterminate all of humanity. Freud's thinking here was reportedly deeply affected by the carnage and hitherto unmatched destruction that he witnessed in World War I. One can apply and follow Freud's thinking in this work, as many highly intelligent people have done in the 20th century. But the results have proven far from spiritually illuminating. The BBC documentary, "The Century of the Self," does an excellent job of portraying this course from Freud to his nephew Edward Bernays, the father of public relations, to Madison Avenue advertisers, to our modern spin doctors. Though brilliant and original, Freud's conception of a 'dark side' appears to have been as accurate as his now mostly discarded notion of the human brain as an appendage of our sexual organs.

It is to Jung that one can turn for a far more fruitful consideration of the "dark side." Jung's creative use of archetypes as metaphors for various psychological phenomena led to many new insights. One of his most powerful metaphors was that of the "Shadow." By this, he meant the autonomous world within. It is not evil, although it may do things that we or others might later judge as evil. In the end, we are wholly accountable for the actions, omissions, and consequences of the Shadow, even if we are

---

[3] Kets de Vries, and Katharina Balazs, "The Shadow Side of Leadership" in <u>The Sage Handbook of Leadership"</u>,ed. Alan Bryman, David Collinson. et.al. (London: Sage Publications, 20011). pp. 138-140.
[4] James Hollis, Why Good People Do Bad Things: Understanding Our Darker Selves. (New York: Gotham Books, 2007). Pp 7-8.

unconscious of its enactments at the time.[5] To use Jung's own words: "The Shadow is a moral problem that challenges the whole ego personality, for no one can become conscious of the Shadow without considerable moral effort. To become conscious involves recognizing the dark aspects of the personality as present and real."[6]

If we are honest with ourselves, very few of us, and especially those we call our leaders, earnestly take on this responsibility and see it through. It takes a very healthy sense of self, and a good deal of courage, to examine and face our "darker selves," our splinter selves and complexes. It is so much easier to deny, rationalize, avoid, blame others, project elsewhere, or bury it, and just keep on rolling. Yet, it is at these moments of human frailty and inadequacy when we are most dangerous to ourselves, our families, and to society at large. Facing our Shadows is not an act of self-indulgence but a way of taking responsibility for our choices and their consequences. It also takes an enormous sense of humility to realize that there is more within each of us than we can ever make conscious and assimilate. Our great spiritual teachers down through the ages have known this, and one of their tasks has been to remind us of that. They ask us, do we repress what lurks in our basement, or project the darkness unto others?[7] Think of all the darkness projected by an unemployed Austrian artist in a book he wrote and whose title in English translates as "My Struggle." Looked at objectively today, which is indeed difficult given the enormous destruction he unleashed in the Second World War, one can see a tormented soul overwhelmed by some very dark and insidious Shadows.

It is not just our psychologists, psychotherapists, and psychiatrists who have recognized and told us of our "Shadows." Our historians, novelists, playwrights, and poets, sometimes

---

[5] Ibid. p. xii.
[6] Ibid. p.5.
[7] Ibid. pp. 5-6.

unknowingly, have spoken of them for centuries. Think of the plays of Sophocles and Aristophanes, or Shakespeare's tragedies and histories. The great 20th-century poet, A. H. Auden, in his poem, "September 1, 1939," also mentions it:

> I and the public know
> What all schoolchildren learn.
> Those to whom evil is done
> Do evil in return.

We would therefore be remiss not to remember that our artists, through their works, reflect back to us the eternal truths of our lives and their hidden meanings. Since we make it so difficult to survive as a truth teller, and our graveyards are full of leaders who died prematurely for their transforming leadership efforts, our artists may be all we can ultimately count on to fulfill this vital and difficult task. If there is any doubt on that score, one only has to read what Ronald Heifetz has had to say on the subject of assassination of leaders in his work, Leadership Without Easy Answers. Our artists have an advantage over a leader by being able to cloak and disguise these truths in their works. Thus, they survive and can live to pass on to others through their artistic expressions what they have learned and observed in our leaders.

The Meaning of the Dark Side for Leaders: Choosing the path less taken

We must constantly ask ourselves, what kind of leaders do we want? In the words of Terrence McKenna, "We are led today by the least amongst us, the least intelligent, the least visionary, and the least noble." Is this what we really want? The least? Why not demand the very best? Why have so many of our leaders disappointed us? It is argued here that one of the chief reasons is because we get so many incomplete people. What we need are people who are whole and completed, and to become whole, one must have confronted one's shadow, or dark side. From both a material as well as spiritual perspective, there are incalculable costs and consequences for us when we get a leader who has not done this inner work and grappled with his or her Shadow.

In seeking out the best people to become our leaders, it is not too much to expect that they are familiar with the law of unintended consequences. One's failure to confront one's Shadow can lead to many unintended consequences. According to Jung, one's Shadow is a reflection of the unlived life. That which is unlived creates a divided human soul, half of which remains unconscious and therefore dangerous to one's self and others. Those who take the time and trouble to stop, look, and ask why become more attuned to their own psychological processes. They are courageous and intelligent enough to ask what role their unconscious is playing in their lives. As a result, their lives grow more interesting to them, and potentially more fulfilling. Most importantly, they become less dangerous to themselves and others.[8] Inevitably, then, the law of unintended consequences plays a far less destructive role in their lives.

A decision to ask why and look within is rare in modern Western societies, where worshipping Mammon and the gods of technology has become so common. Appearances, images, and perceptions that are often controlled and manipulated focus our conscious minds on the external, the immediate, and the transitory. We are truly fearful of making the darkness conscious. To do so, as Jung put it, "is disagreeable and unpopular."[9] Not only do we thereby sever our connection to our souls, to our higher selves, but to everything around us, our families, communities, and the natural world of which we are a part. According to some of our environmental scientists, we may soon become an endangered species, and yet we act as if we do not even know it, or in a state of

---

[8] Ibid. p. xii.
[9] Ibid. Forward).

denial, act as if we do not even care about it. As humans, we are becoming mere appendages of our machines and artificially intelligent-driven technologies. Obi-Wan's description of Vader as "more machine than human" is a predictive metaphor that is awaiting us should we choose not to deal with our Shadows.

If failure to face one's shadows exacts a high price from us as individuals, it is exponentially so when it is a leader. What is denied within us will eventually be visited upon the world, sooner or later, in the guise of fate:

> To be possessed by the Shadow is to bring large energy into the world. No wonder it is so often so seductive. Sometimes we are left to pick up the pieces; other times, others have to pick up the pieces for us. And none of us is more dangerous than the righteous who uncritically believe they are right, for they are the least capable of knowing the harm they bring with them into this world. Was it not an American major standing amid the rubble of the Vietnamese village of Bien Tre who said, "We had to destroy this village in order to save it." He saw no contradiction of values. Again, one of the surest signs of being possessed by the Shadow is the ready rationalizations we have to make them palatable to our conscience.[10]

The point here is that when our leaders fail to live out their unlived lives, their personal shadows take over. That which they kept at bay and suppressed or ignored since its inception might prove costly to their numerous adaptations, a threat to their ego's survival. Perhaps that is why the old cliché that we become our own worst enemies is so often true.[11] One can see this when we avoid, repress, split off, project onto others, and rationalize our selfish, harmful behavior. These are elemental and primitive defenses against what

---

[10] Ibid. p. 20.
[11] Ibid. p. 55.

we believe or feel will threaten our insecure and immature egos.[12] When our leaders succumb to these dysfunctional responses, we do not get very effective or constructive leadership. In fact, we may get very catastrophic leadership.

It is an old truism that no one can be a leader without followers. Leaders are not solo pilots. They need colleagues, partners, and companions in order to accomplish their and their organization's goals. So those whom leaders choose to surround themselves with can have a massive effect on what they accomplish, whether it be good or bad. Our less complete and less wholesome leaders will make all manner of mistakes here. They may unconsciously choose sycophants, enablers, servile, manipulative, or deviant types to work with. We forget at our peril that a leader's ability to weigh and size people up is crucial to his or her success. What is less commonly talked about is how this crucial task can come undone. A man or woman who has not recognized and dealt with his or her own shadows within will never be able to recognize them in another. They are therefore Jungian vulnerable to being blindsided when it comes to recognizing the hidden psychological foibles, conflicts, and problems of subordinates whose contributions they, by necessity, must rely upon. All manner of unintended consequences, mostly negative, will happen to them as the outside world surrounding them reflects back to them their incomplete and unrecognized shadows.

There are far too many reasons for our failure to face our shadows to list here. Two, however, stand out. The first arises from the ego, which is less than thrilled when it confronts the Shadow. No one is perfect, and none of us could survive without a considerable capacity for adaptation. Our adaptations allow us to take on the values, messages, and reflexes of our environment, to internalize family dynamics and cultural beliefs and practices. They make it possible to meet our physical and emotional needs and survive.

---

[12] Ibid. pp. 24-25.

Without them, we risk becoming alienated from our social connections.[13] Unfortunately, our pathologies, neuroses, addictions, sociopathies, which are really expressions of suffering, are also products of our adaptations. With each adaptation, we become further estranged from our souls.[14] When our egos over-identify with our adaptations, it is easier to hide in a state of denial than take up the confrontational struggle that may take years to work through. Nor can we expect that this work can be done without some suffering. The poet Robert Browning Hamilton had a few eloquent words to say about this in one of his poems:

> I walked a mile with Pleasure,
> She chattered all the way,
> But she left me none the wiser,
> For all she had to say.
> I walked a mile with Sorrow,
> And ne'er a word said she;
> But, oh, the things I learned from her
> When Sorrow walked with me!

One of the more obvious expressions of the Shadow phenomena can be seen in a narcissistic personality. According to Jungian Analyst James Hollis, the narcissistic personality is devoted to hiding his or her secret, because when they stare into the mirror, no one stares back. Consequently, they have a constant need to use others in order to elicit positive mirroring, which was sadly deficient when their emerging sense of self was forming. They compensate this need with an inordinate sense of entitlement (the Bathsheba Syndrome), which usually lacks the reciprocity that governs relationships. They fail to empathize with others whom they use, which includes even their own children, to bolster their shaky sense of self. They seek to control, bully, and dominate those close to them. The Shadow issue

---

[13] Ibid. p. 60.
[14] Ibid. p. 61.

for a narcissist is not only the manipulation and misuse of others, but his or her failure to address their inner deficits. These deficits within rob them of the strength necessary to take on the task of working through their shadow issues.[15] How many narcissistic leaders have so many of us seen in politics, religion, business, and governmental affairs? The historical list is endless, and the trail of destruction left behind them horrifying.

The second prominent reason for the failure to deal with one's Shadow arises out of many mainstream Western cultural and religious roots. They are unlike some Eastern theological traditions, which consider the problem of evil as a delusion of the ego. It is the ego's imperial fantasies that are at the root of the problem, as it seeks to separate itself from the flow of life and attempt to expand and swallow the cosmos. Overthrowing the delusions of the ego is the project of both Buddhism and Hinduism. In the Western theological traditions, be it Christian, Jewish, or Muslim, the "other" is pathologized as the Evil One who tempts us to "sin". One can only resist and be "saved" by "good works" or the "grace" of the deity. The nature of many fundamentalist theological expressions is to compound this problem by harassing the ego for more and more control. Such a strategy only drives the Shadow deeper, thereby energizing it, making it even more dangerous.[16] Leaders who are unaware of this can become ensnared in mind games and unconscious forces that will eventually undermine and destroy what they are trying to do. We end up with leaders who disappoint us. We do not see them as people to emulate, or even as lesser mortals with feet of clay, but as tragically flawed and incomplete people who have become leaders not to be of service to others but to serve themselves. They fail not just because of what they are but because they have not accomplished the most basic and fundamental task of a leader, and that is to set an example. They are the ones who often surround

---

[15] Ibid. pp 77-78.
[16] Ibid. pp. 34-35.

themselves with an echelon of courtiers, sycophants, gatekeepers, and public relations hacks to keep the hoi polloi at a distance, lest they see what the emperor is wearing.

Another deficiency of leaders who have not dealt with their shadows is the effect they have on followers. In many organizations, those who rise to the top are men and women whose need for power makes them averse to self-criticism and criticism from others. How many people have the courage to tell the emperor he has no clothes on? Such leaders become resistant to change, genuine dialogue, dissent, and the criticism of those most affected by the common neuroses. The Shadow of any organization is constituted by that which threatens the ego in charge, that which carries the unexamined, the unconsciousness of leadership. Even a benign group can end up being controlled by greed, immaturity, or the narcissistic needs of the boss. The entire group then suffers. The health of an organization is vitally linked to quality of life issues, which are so often ignored and pushed into the Shadow realm by those concerned primarily with the short term.[17] One can see this in so many business organizations that have gone bust in the last decade, such as Enron, Arthur Andersen, Tyco, Lehman Brothers, and many others. A society that massively rewards hedge fund speculators, legalizes financial fraud, launches wars of aggression, justifies austerity on the backs of its most vulnerable, weakest citizens, ignores the environmental destruction of a dysfunctional economic system, is clearly one that has failed to grapple with its collective Shadow. While all bear some responsibility for this, our leaders bear the most.

Making a Friend of the Dark Side

It is suggested here that the human psyche's separation and incompleteness are at the root of our Shadows. Our conscious minds live in a state of denial and can only understand a part of human

---
[17] Ibid. pp. 124-125.

consciousness. As a consequence, the conscious mind can never experience the wholeness and completeness of what human consciousness offers. It is clear that Jung understood this:

> The rupture between faith and knowledge is a symptom of the *split consciousness* which is so characteristic of the mental disorder of our day. It is as if two different persons were making statements about the same thing, each from his own point of view, or as if one person in two different frames of mind were sketching a picture of his experience. If for "person" we substitute "modern society," it is evident that the latter is suffering from a mental dissociation, i.e., a neurotic disturbance.[18]

> For more than fifty years, we have known, or could have known, that there is an unconscious as a counterbalance to consciousness. Medical psychology has furnished all the necessary empirical and experiential proofs of this. There is an unconscious psychic reality which demonstrably influences consciousness and its contents. All this is known, but no practical conclusions have been drawn from it. We still go on thinking and acting as before, as if we were *simplex* and not *duplex*. Accordingly, we imagine ourselves to be innocuous, reasonable, and humane. We do not think of distrusting our motives or of asking ourselves how the inner man feels about the things we do in the outside world. But actually it is frivolous, superficial, and unreasonable of us, as well as psychically unhygienic, to overlook the reaction and standpoint of the unconscious.[19]

More importantly, the unconscious Shadow has been portrayed as a dark pit, a source of pain and suffering. Yet, there is another way of looking at this. In the words of Joseph Campbell, "the Shadow is the landfill of the self. Yet it is also a sort of vault; it holds great,

---

[18] C. G. Jung, The Undiscovered Self (London: Routledge & Kegan Paul, 1958), p. 74.
[19] Ibid. p.84.

unrealized potentialities within."[20] There can be positive outcomes if we truly and courageously face our Shadow. This process requires one to discern what wishes to be expressed through us, and mobilizing the energy and commitment to sustain it. Our positive Shadow, like our dark Shadow, is who we really are. They are one and the same, and not to be split apart as positive and negative aspects of the ego.[21] Looked at from outside the confines of the ego and the conscious mind, there is no split, only a wholeness that we may not yet be aware of.

To reach this level of conscious realization is a journey each person must make. Every journey is unique and in the end solitary. One can find a path in one's dreams, through meditation, reflection, and learning to read the wisdom that is imprinted within.[22] The wisdom of the Buddha ("Heaven lies within, seek it diligently") and the Nazarine ("the Kingdom of Heaven lies within you") proclaimed this eternal truth. But to find this truth out for oneself requires one to take a very different journey than that chosen by most. It requires one to make the strenuous efforts required to break loose from the confines of the ego. Jung's belief was that humanity could best accomplish this by becoming reacquainted with our instincts:

> The forlornness of consciousness in our world is due primarily to the loss of instinct, and the reason for this lies in the development of the human mind over the past aeon. The more power man had over nature, the more his knowledge and skill went to his head, and deeper became his contempt for the merely natural and accidental, for that which is irrationally given – including the objective psyche, which is all that consciousness is not. In contrast to the subjectivism of the conscious mind, the unconscious is objective, manifesting itself mainly in the form of contrary

----

[20] Hollis, p. 183.
[21] Ibid. p. 195.
[22] Ibid. p. 194.

feelings, fantasies, emotions, impulses, and dreams, none of which one makes oneself but which come upon one objectively. Even today, psychology is still, for the most part, the science of conscious contents, measured as far as possible by collective standards. The individual psyche has become a mere accident, a "random" phenomenon, while the unconscious, which can manifest itself only in the real, "irrationally given" human being, has been ignored altogether. This was not the result of carelessness or of lack of knowledge, but of downright resistance to the mere possibility of there being a second psychic authority besides the ego. It seems a positive menace to the ego that its monarchy can be doubted.[23]

Perhaps it might be helpful to see the Shadow as an expression of the will of the Gods, in spite of the discomfort it causes our nervous systems. (Hollis, p. 194)[24] To the ancient Greeks, the word "hubris" meant failure to listen to the Gods. Therefore, listening to them, which is so hard for the ego to do, can lead one to see the Shadow not as an enemy but as a friend. In life, our truest and best friends are the ones who have the courage to tell us the truth, not the ones who tell us what we want to hear. Those who have experienced hubris have not yet faced their Shadow and made a friend of the one who will tell them the truth.

Life's events eventually force each of us at some point to ask, who am I, and why am I here? We will not find the answers to those spiritual questions until we are obliged to reach and search within to draw upon the resources nature has given us.[25] This is one of the meanings of "the hero's journey' that our great artists have spoken of. It is a journey to discover the divine characters lying dormant within our souls. In their book, Romancing the Shadow, Connie

---

[23] Jung, pp. 85-86.
[24] Hollis, p.194.
[25] Hollis, p. 194.

Zweig and Steve Wolf express the real meaning and purpose of shadow work:

> We have tried to show that the shadow is not an error, a failure, or a flaw. It is part of our nature, a portion of the natural order of who we are. And it is not a problem to be solved: it is a mystery to be faced. The Shadow connects us to our own imaginal depths. Shadow work fuels our creativity, which in turn frees us from the grips of an archetype. And shadow work links us with the ancestors and the unborn, and the commons, and with other species.

Romancing the shadow is not a way to slay the shadow; it's not a heroic gesture, a killing off of a monstrous part of ourselves. And romancing the shadow is not a way to harness the beast to do the ego's work. Instead, it's a way of being with a part of ourselves that is repulsive or grotesque. It's a way to witness it, be present for it, and understand it; but, more deeply, it's a way to honor it. As Christ could not complete his destiny without the betrayal of Judas, as Faust could not complete himself without the encounter with Mephistopheles, so we become who we are through romancing the shadow. That is why we say that shadow work is soul work.[26]

Conclusions

It is submitted here that our leaders, consciously or unconsciously, project their shadow or their light onto all those around them, including their followers and the organizations and communities that they play a role in. A leader shapes the ethos in which others must live, an ethos of light-filled heaven or a shadow-filled hell.[27] Contrary to popular belief, our best leaders do not just

---

[26] Connie Zweig and Steve Wolf, Romancing the Shadow: Illuminating the Dark Side of the Soul (New York: Ballantine Books, 1977), pp. 306-307.

[27] Parker Palmer J. Let Your Life Speak: Listening for the Voice of Vocation (San Francisco: Jossey-Bass, 2000), p. 78.

show us light, but the interplay, the relationships, and eternal truths that flow from both light and darkness. To show us a complete picture, a fulfillment of life's vital forces, a leader must have first looked closely at his or her own shadows, and studied, tamed, and transposed their instinctual natures. Such a leader compels us by their example to look at our own personal and collective shadows, and ask ourselves the difficult questions that our personal and societal growth requires. Such leaders challenge us to change and transform our lives and the world we live in.

In this age where so much emphasis is placed on the external, the surface, and the temporal image, it is easy to be fooled by charismatic and extroverted leaders. Such persons make it difficult for others to recognize their shadows. Extroversion can also be a useful technique to hide and cope with self-doubt and anxiety, and charisma can be a very dangerous source of power over others.[28] Is it any wonder that acting skills are now considered by some to be an important part of a leader's toolkit? Those who have done their Shadow work, however, can see through the act, the hypocrisy, and phoniness. Unfortunately, those who have not done it are often vulnerable and fooled. We have all seen, read about, or heard of messianic leaders who showed us how well the road to hell is paved with good intentions.

The unhappiest and most tragic effect of those leaders whose shadow work is unfulfilled or incomplete is on the personal level. It is the separation they experience from their higher selves, or souls. Only complete persons who have done their light and shadow work can become the authentically healthy, courageous, and visionary leaders the world so desperately now needs. To some, it may appear elitist, even undemocratic, to argue for such leaders, but it is also a rational and noble desire to want such leaders. After all, if we are to be led by anyone, should it not by the best of us, those whom

---

[28] Ibid. p. 86.

Thomas Jefferson referred to as our natural aristocracy? Such individuals will be those who choose not to lead from places of fear and ignorance, but from places of hope, integrity, and trust.

It is submitted here that Carl Jung probably best among our contemporaries understood the integration of the 'dark side'. David Tacey, who has written many books on Jung, has clearly and concisely expressed Jung's thinking as follows:

> "Certainly the most important act for the future is to become aware of our darkness, lower our moral sights, resist the desire to be perfect, recognize our complexity, become critical of conventional morality, and search for a new balance that includes the dark as well as the light. Such psychological development, Jung believed, starts with individuals who have the courage to accept their personal darkness, and it moves out from there to the social sphere. He was pessimistic about such change originating from above, by government decree or religious ideologies, and felt true change begins from below. For Jung, contemplating evil is a practical necessity. The dark side has the power to destroy or transform us. If we do not accept the challenge of consciousness, destruction is inevitable. If we move to the dark side with respect and awareness, it will transform us. How we choose to respond will determine which fate awaits us."[29]

One last word here for the wise. Recalling Luke's descent into the cave, it is worth remembering that both before and after his experience, his guide and mentor, Yoda, was there to help him make sense of what he experienced. So, before you confront your 'Shadow', be warned. You might be wise to listen to your 'guides' or mentors, or you may end up where Luke's father did, best described by Nietzsche:

---

[29] David Tacey, <u>The Darkening Spirit: Jung Spirituality Religion</u> (New York; Routledge, 2013), p.106.

"He who fights too long with dragons, becomes a dragon himself; and if thou gaze too long into the abyss, the abyss will gaze into thee."

REFERENCES

Burns, James MacGregor. *Leadership*. New York: Harper & Row, 1978.

Heifetz, Ronald A. *Leadership Without Easy Answers*. Cambridge: The Belknap Press, 1994.

Hollis, James. *Why Good People Do Bad Things: Understanding Our Darker Selves*. New York: Gotham Books, 2007.

Jung, C. G. *The Undiscovered Self*. London: Routledge & Kegan Paul, 1958.

Kellerman, Barbara. *Bad Leadership: What it is, How it Happens, Why it Matters*. Boston: Harvard Business School Press, 2004.

Kellerman, Barbara. *The End of Leadership*. New York: HarperCollins, 2012.

Kets de Vries, and Balazs, Katharina. "The Shadow Side of Leadership." In Alan Bryman, David Collinson, Keith Grint, Brad Jackson, and Mary Uhl-Bien (editors), *The Sage Handbook of Leadership*. London: Sage Publications, 2011.

Lipman-Blumen, Jean. *The Allure of Toxic Leaders: Why We Follow Destructive Bosses and Corrupt Politicians – and How We Can Survive Them.*
New York: Oxford University Press, 2005.

Palmer, Parker J. *Let Your Life Speak: Listening for the Voice of Vocation*. San Francisco: Jossey-Bass, 2000.

Robertson, Robin. *From the Inside Out: Mining the Soul*. York Beach, Maine: Nicholas Hays, 2000.

Robertson, Robin. *The Shadow's Gift: Find Out Who You Really Are*. York Beach, Maine, 2011.

Tacey, David. *The Darkening Spirit: Jung, Spirituality, Religion*. New York, Routledge, 2013.

Zweig, Connie, and Wolf, Steve. *Romancing the Shadow: Illuminating the Dark Side of the Soul*. New York: Ballantine Books, 1977.

Chapter Four

The Light Side

The Inner Mind of Our Rulers

If you want to govern the people,
You must place yourself below them.
If you want to lead the people,
You must learn how to follow them.

The Master is above the people,
And no one feels oppressed
She goes ahead of the people,
And no one feels manipulated.
The whole world is grateful to her.
Because she competes with no one,
No one can compete with her.

Lao Tzu, "Tao Te Ching" (Verse 66)

Alas, the question remains. Is there a way out of this human dystopia so far described, that the psychopaths have led us to? Are there leaders who can do this who have not yet emerged? If so, what will they look like? How will society have to evolve to permit this to happen? Our current 'rulers' have proven not only morally bankrupt and incompetent, but deeply corrupt and no longer fit to rule, let alone serve as 'leaders' for the ruling classes.

One could spend days dissecting, decoding, and deconstructing Yuval Harari's dystopian, Orwellian, technocratic diatribe against everything human in speeches at the WEF and elsewhere. Yet, his views represent the official narrative that governments and corporations, especially Big Tech, have consciously and surreptitiously subjected humanity via indoctrination. To resist this entrainment requires making an effort to proactively seek out and expose oneself to information and perspectives that challenge the ideas and values expressed by these entities. Only then can one gain a more objective, balanced, and credible understanding of the world. At this stage, a more rewarding exercise will be replacing our current 'elite' rulers with people who will prevent this dark scenario from happening. To address this, one first needs to make a journey into the inner minds of those who would choose to rule and lead their fellow humans. Why have so many of our 'rulers' and leaders have failed us? Is there something mentally different about them?

To do this, exploring the mind will take a different approach by looking at it from a left-brain, right-brain, or whole-brain perspective. The imbalances here, it is submitted, directly impact the quality, integrity, and ethical stability of our rulers and leaders. Here, the works of Julian Jaynes and Iain McGilchrist stand out in a numinous and spectacular way.

In his work, *The Origin of Consciousness in the Break Down of the Bicameral Mind*, Jaynes took a radical approach and challenged the mainstream assumptions of 20th-century research, especially with respect to the origins of consciousness in evolution. He also challenged those behaviourists who had solved the problem of consciousness by ignoring it. Jaynes claimed people were confusing consciousness with perception. He researched the ancient texts and hypothesized that the ancient minds were distinctly different from the modern human mind.

They were bicameral. The two hemispheres of the cerebral cortex were organized differently in the past. He used the word bicameral to describe a mental state in which the experiences and memories of the right hemisphere of the brain are transmitted to the left hemisphere via auditory hallucinations. That is, each half of the brain is constantly communicating with the other.

Jaynes theorized that the human brain existed in a bicameral state until as recently as 3000 BC. People, speculated Jaynes, would hear 'voices' from the right brain counterparts to the left brain language centers. These regions are somewhat dormant in the right brains of most modern humans, whose brains are now left-hemisphere controlled, especially since the time of Plato. This has been to our detriment.

Another more prescient and prolific writer on this topic is neuroscientist and philosopher Iain McGilchrist, who laid out his thoughts in his work, *The Master and His Emissary: The Divided Brain and the Making of the Western World*. He has recently added to this work a massive two-volume study of the subject, *The Matter with Things*, which greatly expands Jaynes' theories into practically all aspects of Western civilization with his hemispheric hypothesis. The 'Master' is the right hemisphere of the brain, and the emissary is the left hemisphere. The right brain deals with empathy and intersubjectivity, or the ground of consciousness, the importance of an open patient attention to the world, the emphasis on process rather than stasis (being static), and the journey being more important than the arrival. In truth, it opens the door to the numinous. Its focus is the primacy of perception, the importance of the body in constituting reality and creativity as an unveiling process rather than a wilfully constructive process.[1] More importantly, if the detached, highly focused attention of the left hemisphere is brought to bear on living

----
[1] Ilain McGilchrist, The Master and His Emissary (Yale University Press, 2009), p. 177.

things and not later resolved into the whole picture by right hemisphere attention, which yields depth and context, then it is highly destructive.[2]

Another way of picturing this is to recognize, according to McGilchrist, that feelings come first and reason emerges from it. Our emotions have taught us to reason. The major difference between the two hemispheres lies in their relationship with the unconscious mind, whether that being in the dream state, or what we experience or bear in mind without being aware of it.[3] It is crucial to remember that the right brain hemisphere succeeds in bringing us in touch with whatever is new by an attitude of receptive openness to what is. This contrasts with the left hemisphere's view that it makes new things active by putting them together bit by bit. This can be seen as another example of where the right hemisphere is more true to the nature of things.[4]

McGilchrist does recognize that the left hemisphere knows things the right hemisphere does not, just as the right knows things of which the left is ignorant.[5] However, the generation of the greatest feats of the human spirit requires the integration of both hemispheric worlds. So, a split-brain person often appears to have an impoverished level of imagination and creativity.[6] The left hemisphere often sees the workings of the right hemisphere as purely incompatible, antagonistic, and a threat to its domination. The left hemisphere, the Emissary, perceives the Master, the right hemisphere, to be a tyrant. This is a strange inversion to be sure when you truly understand the role and purpose of the right hemisphere. However, it is an inevitable consequence that the left hemisphere can only support a

---

[2] Ibid. p. 182.
[3] Ibid. p. 187.
[4] Ibid. p.198.
[5] Ibid. p.199.
[6] Ibid. p 198.

machine-like, mechanistic view of the world. So the unifying tendencies of the right hemisphere, which views everything as interconnected, thinks holistically and contextually, and is constantly flowing and exploring, challenging and reversing the left brain's achievements in delineating individual entities.[7]

McGilchrist believes the right hemisphere does not know what the left hemisphere does, for that would destroy its ability to understand the whole. The same applies to the left hemisphere. It cannot know what the right hemisphere knows because, from its perspective, what it has mentally created is complete. Because what the left brain produces is in focus and at the centre of the field of vision, it is more easily seen, and this is one reason why we are more aware of what it contributes to our knowledge of the world. It cannot, however, deliver anything directly new from the outside; it only unpacks what it is given. This is its enormous strength, which is that it can render explicit what the right hemisphere has to leave implicit. Conversely, this is also its weakness. Its clarifying explicitness requires integration with the sense of the whole to have any value and meaning to humanity.[8]

To be more precise, the left hemisphere is competitive, and its concern, its prime motivation, is power. What would the world be like if the left hemisphere appeared to have primacy or became the end point or final staging post on the processing of experience? McGilchrist believes the world would be relatively mechanical, an assembly of more or less disconnected parts. It would be relatively abstract and disembodied, distanced from fellow feeling, given to explicitness, utilitarian in ethics, overconfident of its own views of reality, and lacking insight into the human condition.[9]

---

[7] Ibid. p. 206.
[8] Ibid. p. 208.
[9] Ibid. p. 209.

The right hemisphere deals with our passions, our sense of humour, all metaphoric and symbolic understanding, all religious sense, and all imaginative and intuitive processes. Hence, the relationship between the hemispheres is highly significant for the type of world in which we live.[10] The right hemisphere 'looks out' for both hemispheres' territory, not just its own, like the left hemisphere. In the competition between the two, the left hemisphere has a greater suppressive effect on the right than the reverse. And so, the direction of influence tends to be more that of the left over the right. The two sides, however, need and depend on one another.[11] Though McGilchrist sees the left hemisphere as having a valuable role, its processes need to be returned to the realm of the right hemisphere and once more integrated into a new whole greater than the sum of its parts. But he recognizes that the left hemisphere's point of view will inevitably dominate because it is most accessible, closest to the self-aware, self-inspecting intellect. Language, logic, and linearity all ultimately come under the control of the left hemisphere. So, the cards are heavily stacked in its favour in our conscious discourse and enforcing its worldview. Its point of view is always easily defensible because it is analytic, though it cannot deal very well with paradox and ambiguity.[12]

At some point, one has to ask, given this hemispheric dichotomy, which side controls the human race? Are predominately left-brained or right-brained people in control? Why are there so few humans with balanced, hemispheric, synchronized brains? McGilchrist maintains that the left hemisphere, with its 18th-century model of mechanistic reductionism and scientific materialism, has largely dominated the West. As a result, we have systematically misunderstood the

---

[10] Ibid. p. 209.
[11] Ibid. p. 218.
[12] Ibid. p. 228.

nature of reality. It has actively damaged, physically, the natural world and psychologically, morally, and spiritually hurt humanity as part of that world, and in the process, endangering everything we should value. It posits that the cosmos is a purely material machine, which is, in principle, fully comprehensible by analysis of its parts. It is determined rather than freely creative. He uses the metaphor of a map that symbolizes the left hemisphere. The map contains some truths, but they are very limited in comparison with the understanding of the right hemisphere. A map does contain some truth, but unless you can interpret it in the light of real-world experience, it is useless. Although the map depends on the world, the world does not depend on a map.[13]

McGilchrist also acknowledged that both hemispheres are needed to function as human adults. We do nothing really well with one hemisphere, as many brain-damaged patients have shown us. It may not be a coincidence that babies and young children are more reliant on their right hemisphere, which matures earlier than the left. The increasing importance of the left hemisphere is likely a function of aging, and this process necessitates the separation of the two hemispheres' areas of interest and their realms of activities. He also believes that the left hemisphere's dominance may end up creating what Carl Jung referred to as rationalistic hubris. The growing influence and impact of supercomputers, alternative intelligence, robotization, internet algorithms, smart machines, and many other new technologies look suspiciously tyrannical and dehumanizing. And they are obviously products almost exclusively of the left brain. Ironically, some of the greatest scientific minds, like Einstein, freely admitted that it was their right hemisphere that led to their greatest breakthroughs. The right brain struggles to be heard, as what it knows is too complex, too intuitive, too esoteric, and too far removed from day-to-day activities. Nor has it the advantage of having been

---

[13] Iain McGilchrist, <u>The Matter With Things, Volume II</u> (Perspectiva Press, London, 2021), p. 1306.

carved up into pieces that can be neatly strung together.[14] Is it any wonder that so many of our great artists were misunderstood?

What is not fully appreciated is that it is the right brain which has the most and easiest access to one's unconscious mind. The consequences of this are profound and earth-shattering, for it means that a human being's access to this part of his mind is precluded, if not diminished, if the left brain or emissary is in control. Here is one consequence pointed out by Gustave Le Bon in his well-known work, *The Crowd*, in which he pointed out that many are persuaded by illusions, not logical reasoning. Reasoning is a nullity in its influence on the crowd, who can only be influenced by their unconscious sentiments.[15] Affirmation of this phenomenon can be seen in the oratory powers of Adolf Hitler and his impact on the German people in the 1930s. Now, combine those skills with the power of the modern news media, the internet, and current technology, and you can see the seeds of nascent totalitarianism.

Moreover, as discussed earlier in this work, it has been said that the "shadow" represents the repressed unconscious or the darker aspects of one's personality. Without the ability to see, deal with, and heal it, by having access to one's unconscious, one's ability to lead and become a full and healthy human being is seriously impaired. Significantly, to assume a 'leadership' role makes such a person dangerous to themselves and others, as they will project their darkness onto everyone else.

In connection with this line of thought, McGilchrist also believes the right hemisphere plays a superior role in making moral judgments. He and David Hecht of University College

---

[14] Iain McGilchrist, The Master and His Emissary, p. 229.

[15] Gustave Le Bon, The Crowd: A Study of the Popular Mind (Bibliobazaar LLC, Charleston, S.C.) p. 92.

London both believe that the right hemisphere plays an important role in our ability to distinguish right from wrong. It partakes in assessing the morality of actions, moral reasoning, and promoting prosocial norms. The left hemisphere plays a role in fostering antisocial behaviour. The right hemisphere is also correlated with altruistic tendencies, as well as a sense of fairness. Issues of morality depend on what is going on in another person's mind, and people with damaged right hemispheres often exhibit the characteristics of a psychopath who cannot pick up indirect expressions, hints, tone of voice, irony, facial expressions, body language and all the other ways we tend to infer what is going on in another person's mind, which could be very different from what they are saying. The right hemisphere is responsible for inhibition, the necessary counterpart to emotional, intellectual, and spiritual health. As McGilchrist puts it, "It seems to me that the key role of the right hemisphere in making sure that a response is appropriate in context implies just such capacity to inhibit. Interestingly, in the light of the greater contribution made to intelligence by the right hemisphere, inhibitory control is more efficient in those of higher intelligence."[16]

To summarize McGilchrist's insights, the left hemisphere excels at understanding quantity better than quality. It produces a 'representation' of the world as opposed to a direct experience. It is good at deconstructing. It is outcome-focused. It seeks to grasp things and manipulate them. It sees the world as minutely detailed, abstract, inanimate, and explicit. It wants something certain, static, and familiar, and is out there and known. It is considerably more prone to settle for quick and dirty approaches (heuristics). When urgent, target-oriented action is even contemplated, the left brain is activated, so the left brain is prone to make swift judgements and stick to them unreasonably. Obviously, there are circumstances when

----

[16] Iian McGilchrist, <u>The Matter with Things</u>, Vol. II, pp. 1343-1345.

this may be appropriate. It knows we have to get things to eat to survive, so its concern is how to eat without getting eaten.

Summarizing McGilchrist's insights into the right hemisphere yields perhaps the most profound and discerning observations, as they are often neglected and ignored. It seeks to understand reality and how we construct the world we experience. For it, nothing is certain or separate, as things are flowing and changing all the time. It has the ability to read between the lines as it can take the implicit and see the meaning of what is not being said. It is wide open yet vigilant and plays a crucial role in creativity. It can understand metaphors, analogies, poetry, irony, sarcasm, and music. It is agnostic about what it may find, yet it sees an animated world. It is involved in producing the very presence of something, for example, in a painting, as opposed to the literal picture. It is more guided by intuition and by Gestalt forms. It can appreciate the sense of the beauty of what it is discovering. It is more than just an analytical, procedural way of thinking. Both emotional and social intelligence tend to be more associated with the right hemisphere. With respect to integrating the left and right hemispheres, the right hemisphere is able to use what the left hemisphere knows as well and take it into account. However, the left hemisphere does not seem to be able to take into account what the right hemisphere knows and assumes it is the one that makes things happen. Most importantly, it knows intuitively that the whole is greater than the sum of its parts.

There is little doubt that McGilchrist sees the right brain as superior to the left in its civilizing and evolutionary contribution to human development and our understanding of the cosmos. While both hemispheres contribute, the right hemisphere is superior in every case. Unfortunately, our culture is still dominated by the superannuated 18th-century model of mechanistic reductionism despite our increasing scientific discoveries of quantum physics and a growing understanding of complex systems.[17] This stems from the left hemisphere's dominance and need to control and manipulate, and leads to its intemperate attacks on nature, art, religion, and the human body, which can be seen as the main routes to something beyond the left brain's power.[18] The danger here is that we see the world only in the way the left brain does. We have abandoned our once primal urge to discover the sacred, and our failure to do so will make it increasingly impossible to avoid the downfall and destruction of human civilization. We have become a civilization that is intellectually impoverished, morally bankrupt, and spiritually dead. McGilchrist's warning is ominous: "I was, and am now still more, fearful that unless we *radically* change the path we are pursuing, we cannot survive — certainly as a civilization, and perhaps as a species."[19]

The Balanced Mind of a 21st Century Leader

Historically, we moderns are, in a sense, following the path of other ancient civilizations. In early ancient Greece and ancient Rome, and the early Renaissance periods, our left and right brains were more balanced and supported each other. They enriched and balanced one another. But as time went on, they degenerated to left-brain dominance and became rigid with bureaucratic hierarchies. The flow of ideas, inspiration, intuition, creativity, and innovation all declined as the lust for power, control, and acquisition expanded. Materially, humans were better off, but the seeds of decay and destruction were implanted. In McGilchrist's opinion, the story of the Western World is one of increasing left-hemisphere domination, accompanied by an insouciant optimism, "resembling a sleepwalker

---

[17] Ibid. p. 1306.
[18] McGilchrist, The Master and his Emissary, p 230.
[19] McGichrist, The Matter with Things, Vol II, p. 1312.

whistling a happy tune as he ambles toward the abyss."[20] One can only ask, how much hubris will it take for humanity to wake up?

Already, several characteristics have been noted as desirable for one to be a successful leader in the 21st century, capable of leading humanity from a 3rd dimension reality to one that is more resonant with the highest possibilities of human evolution. One, they cannot be infested with wetico. Only the indigenous people know how to effectively deal with a wetico infestation through banishment. Secondly, if they are psychopaths or have psychopathic tendencies, they must never be allowed to have power over other human beings. People who are psychopaths can be recognized, and if we are courageous and determined, we can prevent them from ever reaching a leadership position. That will take some drastic and dramatic changes in our health and educational institutions. Unfortunately, these systemic changes are far removed from the bureaucratic thought forms and paradigms that currently dominate these institutions. In the meantime, more and more people can be educated and trained to do this in their everyday lives. Learning to shun these psychopaths will be a great start. Thirdly, they must have done some of their own personal but difficult shadow work, learned to deal with their dark side, and transmuted it. Fourthly, as McGilchrist has shown, the brains of our leaders will have to be far more left and right hemisphere balanced. Our current leaders are predominantly left-brained people. One can tell this from the 'fruits' of their labours. Moreover, finding such people amongst our population will not be an easy task. They will not be found in the traditional avenues that people take to become leaders. Many will bear a striking resemblance to the servant leaders that Robert Greenleaf spoke so eloquently about.

---

[20] McGilchrist, The Master and his Emissary, p. 237.

Here are some other complications when the left and right hemispheres are unbalanced, as evidenced when brain damage has occurred. Patients with damage mostly to their left hemisphere reveal greater levels of warmth, sociability, and agreeableness, whereas right hemisphere-damaged patients tend to try and control and dominate: trust, straightforwardness, altruism, compliance, modesty, and tender-mindedness correlate positively with right orbital frontal, and negatively with left orbitofrontal. Significantly, studies of brain-damaged patients have shown that right hemisphere damage can lead to sexual aggression, physical assaults, and acquired psychopathy. Some studies have even shown that when normal subjects were engaged in mental simulations of immoral acts, there was a 'remarkable shift' in their brain activity towards the left hemisphere. David Hecht believes that "these studies suggest that moral and immoral thinking are associated with activity in the right hemisphere and left hemisphere, respectively." The desire for benign social connectedness, agreeableness, and a tendency to trust others all implicate the right hemisphere. A disposition towards gratitude, being appreciative and thankful for the kindness of others, also correlates with the volume of the right temporal cortex.[21]

It is submitted here that the most compelling characteristic of leaders in the 21st century will be their drive and thirst for numinosity that they wish to share with humanity. Here again, McGilchrist has much to tell us. He believes that a disposition towards God is largely dependent on the right hemisphere, the hemisphere that brings us closer to truth than the left. The left, the emissary, has usurped the role of the right as the master. As far as humanity is concerned, the summit of knowing is knowing that you do not know. This has been an expressed conclusion of many highly evolved individuals: the Buddha, Confucius, Socrates, St. Paul, and a great many Indian gurus and saints, all of whom offered the wisdom in valuing not-knowing. This not-knowing is not the same as

----

[21] McGilchrist, The Matter with Things Vol. II, pp.1345-1346.

ignorance. It is what is left in front of us when ignorance is left behind.[22]

True knowing is an experience of *understanding*, a form of perception and appreciation, and not a matter of accumulating facts. It is the difference between seeing things on their surface, as opposed to what is underneath, around, and behind them, as well as their emptiness. To quote Lao Tzu, "To know truth, one must get rid of knowledge; nothing is more powerful and creative than emptiness, from which men shrink." The Buddhist concept of emptiness, or *sunyata*, is related to this. Like a receptive womb, there needs to be a place for the new understanding, the new wisdom to grow. And where there is no room to grow, there can be no receptive womb.[23]

It is the right hemisphere that is better at accepting uncertainty and limits to knowledge. Moreover, an understanding of the divine must rely on indirect and metaphorical expression, not direct and literal expression. It must be able to tolerate ambiguity and be at ease with what appears contradictory and paradoxical. It can see that spirit and body are not distinct, but are different aspects of the same thing. It involves sustaining attention and stilling the inner voice through prayer and meditation. It can recognize, and not deny, the dark side of human consciousness, and be capable of understanding that good may, despite everything, emerge from suffering. In short, there is strong reason to believe that an understanding of the divine is sustained largely through the right hemisphere, and that this hemisphere will play a preeminent role, as Master, in the 21st century.[24]

---

[22] Ibid. p. 1208.
[23] Ibid. pp. 1209.
[24] Ibid. pp. 1210-1211.

What McGilchrist has shown is that a different type of brain can lead humanity to a different destiny, one very different than the one the current left hemisphere domination trajectory is leading. This path will not be without struggle, and there will be, by necessity, a birthing process that needs to take place as it moves from the womb of humanity to various expressions in life. The goal will be a new kind of human whose left and right hemispheres are balanced, unified, and synchronistic. People who are left-brain hemisphere dominant are inclined to hold right hemisphere dominant people in contempt, disbelief, and as naïve dreamers, basically useless, impractical people. Right-brain dominant people see left-hemisphere people as dull, unimaginative, over-materialistic, unfeeling, and lacking in 'spiritual values.'[25]

Since so many people today are left-hemisphere dominant, changing their mindset will not be an easy or quick fix. A return to a more balanced human at this time will necessitate incentives, acknowledgement, and rewards for striving to live as a fully alive human. Activities like making works of art, painting, sculpting, working with handicrafts, gardening, spending more time in nature, playing a musical instrument, composing music, reading, and writing poetry and fictional literature. Other social and educational changes can be made to encourage people to express emotions such as joy and compassion, giving people time to daydream and to appreciate the beauty of form and movement in dancing and acting. In today's economic, social, and political environment, this may seem to be a fantasy since so much of our daily lives are preoccupied with sheer survival. Our lives today are spent working long hours, even taking on more than one job, since one will not allow one to make ends meet. Those who earn large salaries are prisoners of their professions, and the corporations they work for that preclude and hinder the exploration of their right hemispheres. It seems almost a

---

[25] Robert A. Monroe, Ultimate Journey (New York, Harmony Books, 1994), pp. 85-89.

lost cause to change this trajectory and escape McGilchrist's dire predictions.

The key to a reawakening and more balanced life will require a change and expansion of human consciousness. The obvious question, however, is what is consciousness? This question is considered one of the most challenging and pervasive problems in the whole of philosophy. Our own consciousness seems to be the most basic fact confronting us, yet it is almost impossible to say with words what consciousness is.[26] We do know that it has something to do with cerebral activity, with perceptions, thoughts, feelings, in short, with awareness. We also know that it has something to do with preconscious, subconscious, and unconscious mental phenomena, in addition to conscious activities. It is sometimes explained as the medium between the material and the spiritual or unconscious. It is the experiential door to one's higher self through which one can discern a sacred presence. At the simplest level, to try and understand it, when you ask yourself a question, you can ask who is it that is asking the question, who is behind it? What is its source? Some maintain that consciousness is the source from which the question arises.

Expanding our consciousness awareness will open our minds, enabling us to see, understand, and experience much more of the living reality. It has been said that we are at a turning point of consciousness on our little planet. The doors of parapsychology, depth psychology, the paranormal, the mystical, and psychic experience will be opened and change our human experience at such profound levels that we can only fantasize right now. Our minds will be open to the divine as never before. Clairaudience, clairvoyance, claircognizance,

---

[26] Simon Blackburn, The Oxford Dictionary of Philosophy (Oxford, Oxford University Press, 2006), p. 74.

telekinesis, and more will be common experiences, and not just of Hindu saints and yogis who have experienced them for centuries. We may yet realize our destiny as gods and stewards of consciousness. After all, if we are the offspring of gods, does not our legacy lead us to become gods ourselves?[27]

In simple terms, human learning currently, for the vast majority of humans, comes from three or four basic sources. One is through reading and hearing others speak to our conscious minds. Two comes from our lived experiences, things we have done or have happened to us. It is the most common form of human learning. If you have worked and trained to become a doctor, you instinctively know what a doctor is. You have been one, and those life experiences are part of you. When someone refers to a doctor, you know what they mean. You do not have to look it up or ask someone. A third, and perhaps emerging, form of learning, as humans read less and less, is the learning that takes place through social media, electronic devices, and the internet. Most of it is just data, and it is too early to say how far and how deep this learning will take humanity. Also, these forms of communication can only operate within the scope of its fed-in programs and process only those materials of which the programs are capable.[28] A similar restraint exists with artificial intelligence. Fourthly, and perhaps the rarest form of learning, is the knowledge, perceptions, and feelings that one acquires from his or her "higher self" or inner light. Mystics believe that this light stems from the pineal gland in our brains. Most psychologists currently believe this is our subconscious, and being atheists, they cannot see a connection to a divine spark that meditators and users of sacred plant medicines speak of. It requires enormous discipline and training as well as

---

[27] Eva Rider, "Through the Looking Glass: Reflections and Adventures in Social Media" in Depth Psychology & the Digital Age, ed. Bonnie Bright (United States, Depth Insights, 2016), p. 235.

[28] Ingo Swann, Resurrecting the Mysterious (United States, Swann-Ryder Productions, 2020), p. 442.

respect and reverence for the numinous, the spiritual, that is asleep in so many people living on the globe today.

Another way of looking at our planet today is to consider it from an esoteric point of view as a three-dimensional (3D) reality. Think of a dimension as a metaphysical grouping of energy. In a 3D world, our five senses predominate. Life is experienced more densely. Survival and competition created by a Malthusian illusion of scarcity prevail. Illness, pain, trauma, struggling, anxiety, depression, criticism, materialistic focus in manifesting from the earth level, looking outside for love, and no desire to seek within, are all characteristics of our 3D worlds. At its worst, it is a Hobbesian life, being solitary, poor, nasty, brutish, and short. With our current technological capacity to wipe out all life on the planet, it is imperative that humans evolve beyond this primitive dimension. Religious convictions aside, people of sincere heart can find consolation in the conviction that there are powers beyond and above human corruption that govern the destiny of the planet. And in that direction, individuals with a higher consciousness are destined to lead us.

Fortunately, many have woken up to the poverty, life-threatening, and spiritual emptiness of living in a 3D world. Some call it the Great Awakening, aroused largely by the forces of transparency rolling through modern societies through new technologies. Some refer to the *Book of Revelations* in the *Bible*, which they believe is unfolding. To others, it refers to a time of 'revealing' when falsehoods will be exposed and the truth recognized for all to see. Still others refer to 2012, and the Mayan calendar, which predicted the commencement of a new age for humanity. Astrologers, too, have language describing what they believe is going on.

Some of the early aspects of a new age, a 4th-dimensional reality, are emerging for us to see. Human minds are expanding beyond the limits of the five senses. There is more acceptance, compassion, self-love, and a willingness to do shadow work on a personal basis. People are finding that regular jobs don't cut it anymore and desire to find a purpose in their lives. They are seeing the control and lies of the 'rulers' and are more and more irritated by the news, social media, and political world. They desire to work more from their hearts, to find time to be in nature, to notice the beauty around them, and to manifest their dreams. Spiritual archetypes and a growing awareness of the collective mind or unconscious are also becoming real.

What is potentially emerging beyond a 4D reality is an even more advanced and esoteric possibility for humanity. This is what some refer to as 5D, or fifth dimensionality. This is a world that has transformed and evolved into a state never before realized on this planet. Some might think of it as heaven, where pure love and a unity consciousness prevail. Human hearts are fully opened, and a unified healing field exists, so few humans suffer the physical ailments they experience in a 3D world. It is a world where creativity, thriving, cooperation, and manifesting from the heart take place. Wisdom, non-judgement, telepathic communication, a sense of timelessness, and access to many more senses is the norm. Human life is far less physical and dense in its experience, as our bodies are much lighter in shape and felt expression. In other words, physicality will not dominate our lives to the extent it does in 3D. We will live in a more metaphysical society, expressing and experiencing life more abundantly and fluently through our higher selves. When we imagine such a world today, we can think only of an angelic one, not one we mere mortals could ever achieve. Yet, it can and will be our destiny if we choose to make it so.

Possibilities and Opportunities Moving from 3D to 5D Realities

Reaching a 5D reality will take many years of transformation. We are not at this level now, and probably not for the foreseeable future, given so many human limitations that will have to be overcome. What, then, will we have to change and face?

Firstly, humans will have to learn to take responsibility for their lives and what happens to them. Astoundingly, a very tiny group of people, many of them psychopathic in nature, have managed to take control of the lives of over eight billion people. This is a feat that even the ancient emperors of China, Babylon, and Rome would envy. If this tiny elite continues to manage our societies, the movement towards more and more centralization and concentration of wealth and power will continue. International institutions such as the U.N., the World Economic Forum, the Bank of International Settlements, the World Bank, the World Health Organization, and other such entities have fallen under the sway of this tiny group of narcissistic egomaniacs. They have also captured what has come to be known as the 'deep state,' which refers to the real governments behind the frontal face of and formal expressions of government. Few people have a real grasp of the power of intelligence agencies hidden in our governments.

Most importantly, this tiny minority has accomplished this through their control of money and credit via the private banking system. Breaking these strangleholds must and can take place through political and economic decentralization and localization. That will require a political, economic, and social revolution at the level and magnitude of the French Revolution in the 1790s. If history is any guide here, this 'revolution' can be either peaceful or violent. The French people chose the latter, and the chaos that resulted was horrifying. One has to ask, is a peaceful path possible?

For there to be a peaceful revolution, an evolutionary leap in the consciousness of humans will be necessary, especially given our fight-or-flight instincts. If humanity can grow out of its reliance on oligarchic and monarchical forms of government, then such a revolution could take place. It would, by necessity, resemble a transformation to the more honest and successful democracies in our past, even though they have been few and far between. As of today, there are precious few examples in our modern world. It has been said that there is no democracy for enlightened beings. Such people are today viewed as weird and different. But, what if we did have such a society? One might well conclude that such a society would not need leaders or, for that matter, much government at all. Yet, the complex, numerous, and varied human relations would certainly compel some means of structuring human affairs. If not, even such an enlightened society would be in a state of anarchy.

One definition of anarchy is a utopian society of individuals who enjoy complete freedom without government. How long would such a 'libertarian' society persist or survive? It is hard to believe, at this time, how such a society could come into being, let alone survive for any length of time, on a planet with eight billion people. Robert Greenleaf once said, we could eradicate all evil on the planet, but within a generation, it would be back. "Granting that fewer evil, stupid, or apathetic people or a 'better' system might make the job easier, their removal would not change matters, not for long. The latter society will come, if it comes, with plenty of evil, stupid, apathetic people around and with an imperfect, ponderous, inertia-charged "system" as the vehicle of change. Liquidate the offending people, radically alter or destroy the system, and in less than a generation, they will all be back."[29]

---

[29] Robert Greenleaf, <u>The Servant as Leader</u> (Indianapolis, Robert K. Greenleaf Center, 1991), pp. 34-35.

If we cannot have a democracy of enlightened beings, what can we have in a 3rd or 4th dimensional world? Is it possible for a whole society to ascend to a 5D reality? Firstly, one needs to know what one means when they refer to "democracy"? To put it succinctly, it means and refers to "self-government" and not a society ruled by oligarchs. As Harold Waldwin Percival has said, government is the authority, administration, and method by which a body or state is ruled. Only in a libertarian dream society is this not so. Real democracy exists and begins at the micro or individual level: "Self-government as applied to the individual, therefore, means that one's feelings and desires, which are or may be inclined by appetites or emotions and prejudices and passions disrupt the body, will be restrained and governed by one's better feelings and desires which think and act according to rightness and reason as standards of authority within, instead of being controlled by the preferences for or the prejudices against the objects of the senses as authority from outside the body."

Rightness and reason come from *within*, and the people's representatives must practice self-government and be qualified to do so.[30] This means a different kind of representative, an inner-directed human as opposed to the outer-directed ones we see everywhere today, making their decisions through polls, public relations experts, money lenders, and the most venal and selfish people who control them. Such souls will know and understand human consciousness at a much deeper and more profound level. They will know, as Jung pointed out, that the unconscious is the real source of human consciousness. What Jung discerned is a personal unconscious (also called the subconscious) and the collective unconscious, and only when

---

[30] Harold Waldwin Percival, <u>Democracy is Self Government</u> (Rochester, The Word Foundation, 1952), p. 139.

viewed from a holistic perspective could one better understand the human psyche (soul).

This consciousness is the source of our human capacity for human thought, reasoning, awareness, and feeling. It was Carl Jung who developed a magnificent vision of our human capacity for consciousness and its creative role and meaning. Jung believed that God, or Source, and all of creation laboured through time to bring conscious awareness into the universe, and that it is the role of human beings to carry that evolution forward.[31] This dilemma for us was very profoundly expressed by Ingo Swann several decades ago: "Moderns (humans) only incompletely understand the conscious realm, at least in so far as the greater occult qualities of them are concerned. But occultists and psychologists do agree on two essential principles — that the unconscious realms exist; and that an individual's general well-being depends on how adequately he or she incorporates their elements into conscious understanding, i.e., makes them visible."[32] This is crudely reflected in the Biblical passage, "Unless men see wonders, they shall not believe."

One can speculate or dream that when humans carry this evolution to the less dense 5th dimension, it is highly probable that their left and right brains will be balanced and integrated. It is possible, then, that a new form of 'leadership' could emerge, which could be described as *fractal leadership*. The technical definition of a fractal is a complex, never-ending pattern created by repeating mathematical equations. Fractal patterns are ubiquitous in nature, and as Benoit Mandelbrot put it, "a fractal is a way of seeing infinity." They are a world in a grain of sand. Visually, one sees patterns repeating again and again when looking at a fractal. Every small part resembles the whole.

----

[31] Robert A. Johnson, Inner Work: Using Dreams and Active Imagination for Personal Growth (New York, Harper Collins, 1986), p.6.
[32] Ingo Swann, p. 472.

It is worthwhile to ponder how this term could translate into the world of leaders and leadership thought, being what it is. If each human soul is a fractal, each of us is spiritually a divine spark. All of us together make up a fractal universe, which is one way of visualizing the universe. One could criticize this as justifying a communist, Borg-type of social order, but that would be myopic and simplistic. From a spiritual perspective, each human soul is a fractal of Source. We are all identical from a spiritual perspective. As such, each of us is a leader and has a responsibility to lead. We cannot pass the buck. Whatever happens is not only a reflection of ourselves but an expression of our power, being, and essence. In other words, we are all and each of us a "leader." What happens to one of us happens to all of us. Once we fully grasp this, we will be able to create a true democracy, and not a collection of humans ruled by a selfish, parasitic cabal that runs our lives through various forms of oligarchic institutions, and to whom we have surrendered our personal sovereignty. It is submitted, from where we stand today, that such an order of humanity will require an evolutionary leap to get to a 5th-dimensional world. This will take time, patience, and much more. The transition will be neither fast nor instantaneous.

For a 5th-dimensional reality to emerge from today's heavily laden 3D world, a number of significant changes will have to take place on the planet. Only then can higher consciousness humans emerge in significant numbers, calling it Human 5.0 as a species, to make a difference. Hitherto, the only way for such humans to live, let alone survive, would be in ashrams, monasteries, and spiritual mystery schools where they could live and hide under the radar. They had no choice, as they dealt with the "occult," a word that has so many perverse and pejorative meanings. The word, however, in truth refers to that which is "hidden" or concealed, and that which is abstruse and mysterious and not easily understood. Without some understanding of the occult, it is unlikely one can ever grasp the great spiritual truths and traditions that could lead to a 5th-dimensional world. Those truths have been hidden for a great many reasons from the great mass of humanity. Without this knowledge, one would be forever trapped by religious traditions that have controlled humanity for the last six thousand years and constricted human evolution.

Here are some of the features of a 5th-dimensional world:

1. A decentralized political system that does not devolve into oligarchic, highly centralized political systems controlled by elites. We have had oligarchies who are afraid of people realizing they are divine, peaceful, and generous. That has to change. We do not need governments as much as we now believe.
2. In order for political decentralization to occur, economic decentralization must precede it. Today's gigantic concentration of wealth will be redistributed in a fair, non-exploitative way. People will seek to create wealth without governments or corporate powers controlling or hindering them. Their natural desire to be free without infringing on others will compel this to happen.
3. Humans will become aware and knowledgeable of how to create wealth without robbing other humans or destroying the environment, including all plants and animals.
4. A new form of money will have to emerge and one that is not controlled by a 'cabal' of bankers or special interests who hoard and concentrate their wealth, and who use their concentrated wealth to control the various political systems. This monetary system will not be built on private debt and credit, which has created so much debt slavery. The creation of money will be treated as a public 'trust' and managed by people who are accountable to their fellow humans.

5. Humans will learn to become much more self-sufficient and grow their own food organically. They will learn how to use, repair, and fix their tools and practical means of survival.

6. Land will be widely distributed and owned, so people are not forced to live in megacities with millions of other humans. As such, they will then be able to be closer to nature again.

7. Our educational systems will have to be rebuilt from the ground up. The purpose of our educational systems will be to illuminate the souls of people, to keep right and left hemispheres balanced, and to value the development of character and virtue again. The most important subject that will be taught is ethics, which will be expressed in every subject. We will no longer have an education system that trains 'workers' for the factories or to be the means of profit by exploitative controllers. Children will be encouraged and allowed to study subjects in which they have a natural attraction and innate talent. Trades will flourish, and children will leave school with the skills to be an adult contributor in the society they choose to live in.

8. Our justice system will also have to be rebuilt, and its emphasis will be on morality and ethics, not just laws. It will be reflective of natural law more than rigid statutes and rules.

9. The activity of 'war' will be abhorrent and as obsolete as that of 'slavery' today. It will not be part of human consciousness anymore. Women will play a much greater and significant role in making this possible. The predictive words of Rudolf Steiner, a hundred years ago, are particularly relevant here:

> Feminine spiritual life, whether in a man or woman, projects onto our existence something of the primitive, something elemental. Wherever this contrast between men and women confronts us, we can see it because it expresses itself with uncommon clarity. People who judge everything by externals criticize spiritual science because many women are drawn to it at the present time. They do not comprehend that this is quite understandable simply because the average brain of a man has overstepped the certain average point in evolution. It has

become drier, more wooden, and therefore clings more rigidly to traditional concepts. It cannot free itself of the prejudices in which it is stuck. Someone who is studying spiritual science may, at times, find it difficult that he must use his masculine brain in this incarnation. The masculine brain is stiff, resistant, and more difficult to manipulate than the feminine brain, which can easily overcome obstacles that the masculine brain erects with its density. Hence, the feminine brain can more readily follow what is new in our way of viewing the world. To the extent to which the masculine and feminine principles come to expression in the structure of the human brain can be said for our present time, it is most uncomfortable and unpleasant to be obliged to use a masculine brain. A masculine brain must be trained to work much more carefully, much more radically than the feminine brain.

10. Humanism and not transhumanism will prevail. In the struggle between the 'organic and natural' and the 'silicon and synthetic,' the former will prevail. Technologies will serve humans, not control them. The movement to replace our bodies with synthetics, chemicals in the blood, computer chips in the brain, and artificial intelligence, which steals from our abilities to access our humanness and higher selves, will fail. This, too, will require different and awakened educational and healthcare systems that primarily value our humanness.

11. People will have to develop the courage and backbone to face and clean up the difficult and deeply destructive social disease, wetico, or psychopathy. On a personal level, this also refers to antisocial and narcissistic personality disorders. Unless this disease is eradicated, which often takes place from birth, none of these features will ever emerge or long survive. The scourges of pedophilia, child rape, organ harvesting, sexual slavery, drug addiction, and other satanic practices will continue. They must be eliminated and banished like leprosy. It is naïve to believe humans will gradually just give up these behaviours, and they

will disappear forever. The mythic story of the demise of Atlantis is worth remembering here.

12. Being less dense than humans, lifetimes will exceed 100 or more years. Many diseases that currently plague humanity will disappear as levels of mental stress, discontent, worry, and fear dissipate. New and ancient holistic and natural forms of medicine will emerge and largely replace the drug, surgery and radiation medical treatments of today. Humans will learn to cure themselves.

13. Humanity's ability to make use of the productive forces of nature will far exceed what we can imagine now. Energy shortages will be ancient history as new forms of energy will emerge, such as anti-gravity, zero-point energy, nuclear fusion, and many other sources that will materialize due to our technological prowess. An age of abundance will happen, and battles and wars over resources and scarcity will disappear. Competition over resources will no longer plague humanity.

14. A new philosophy of life will emerge such that people will realize that they have more power within themselves than those permitted to them by various social formats, structures, and systems. Realizing these powers will render them immune to the powers that be that seek to impose tyranny. Moreover, these powers will enable them to transcend their 3D limitations and open their hearts and minds to the eternal, immortal, universal, and infinite, and to live in light, fearlessness, and unconditional love. This will be the new human 'religion' recognized by all.

Not all these will come to pass at once. It will take decades for most, if not all, to happen. Generations of humans will have to come and go. However, unless these developments happen, it will not be possible for very many 5D leaders to emerge. One can see what will happen to them by looking at what those few brave souls, light leaders, have experienced in the last several thousand years. Think of the tragic fates of Socrates, Jesus, Gandhi, Martin Luther King, and many others who were crucified, murdered, or assassinated by ignorant mobs, blinded by their dark-sided rulers. This is the conundrum facing humanity. How many souls of the 8 billion current inhabitants on this planet would choose to incarnate now without all the restrictions that a 3D world imposes on them? How many would come if there were no wars, diseases, murders, thievery, and all the horrible difficulties and unpleasant, painful occurrences that plague humans? Without experiencing them, life here would be too boring for them. We incarnate now to learn how to transcend these restrictions, as difficult as it may seem, and evolve to a higher level of consciousness. This entails a belief in reincarnation and redemption, which many in the West and Christianized lands do not yet accept. The good news, however, is that human consciousness has risen perceptibly everywhere on the planet. The world events that the evil elites have instigated, such as 9/11, the Iraq wars, financial bankruptcy, Covid 19, have rebounded in the elites' faces. People no longer trust the messengers of falsehoods, the political thespians, and the bankers who run the show behind the veil.

This rise in consciousness will continue until we have the ability to know what others are thinking, not only at a personal or private level but intellectually and cooperatively. We will recover the lost art and skill of communicating telepathically with animals that we once had, and that only indigenous people have retained. Large, complex human organizations that are now dysfunctional with politics, manipulation, and power obsessions will become more organic and work better as humans coalesce and communicate as never before. By organic, one can think comparatively of the cellular structure in a human body. Trillions of cells coordinate automatically. Each cell knows what the other is doing, and there is a chemical and electrical balance that occurs. They all try to balance together, and the new organization has coalescence and coherence. They all have the same information and intelligent goal: to create a healthy human body for as long as possible. This human being has intelligently evolved over hundreds of thousands of years. This is a spiritual intelligence manifesting that continues every moment of our lives and will someday soon produce a healthy human society, functioning with managerless cooperation.[33]

The interregnum period between today's 3D world and a 5D world sometime in the future will have various characteristics that will allow a new generation of leaders to emerge, whose values will reflect the fifth dimension. Many of the mainstream institutions will devolve and gradually disappear. People who have feared stepping forth will find the courage to do so politically and socially. Political parties will disappear, and new ones will emerge. A natural elite of talent and virtue will gradually replace the parasites and psychopaths who 'rule' our societies. As human consciousness evolves, those who have the courage to speak truth to power will no longer hide or fear censorship and repercussions. Manipulative and gatekeeper skills will be deplored and no longer rewarded, as in so many institutions today. What will matter is whether you have integrity, know and speak the truth, and can produce results. You will have done the hard but necessary work to heal your 'shadow.' You are not as dense a person as so many are today. You can access your higher self and have demonstrated that in your day-to-day life. This will seem to many like a long, dark tunnel, but there is a numinous world at the end of it if we have the courage to make it happen in this period of ascension.

----

[33] Lee Carroll, Kyron: The New Human; The Evolution of Humanity (U.S.A., The Kyron Writings Inc., 2017), pp.156-158.

REFERENCES

Blackburn, Simon. The Oxford Dictionary of Philosophy. New York: Oxford University Press, 1994.

Bright, Bonnie, ed. Depth Psychology & the Digital Age. United States: Depth Insights, 2016.

Lee Carroll. The New Human: The Evolution of Humanity, Kryon Book 14. San Diego: The Kryon Writings, Inc., 2017.

Greenleaf, Robert. The Servant as Leader. Indianapolis: The Robert K. Greenleaf Center, 1970.

Jaynes, Julian. The Origin of Consciousness in the Breakdown of the Bicameral Mind. New York: Houghton Mifflin Company, 1976.

Johnson, Robert A. Inner Work: Using Dreams and Active Imagination for Personal Growth. New York: HarperCollins, 1986.

Jung, C.G. Modern Man in Search of a Soul. Eastford, CT: Martino Fine Books, 2021.

Le Bon, Gustave. The Crowd. Charleston, SC: Bibliobazaar.

McGilchrist, Iain. The Matter with Things: Our Brains, Our Delusions and the Unmaking of the World. Volume One: The Ways to Truth. London: Perspectiva Press, 2021.

McGilchrist, Iian. The Matter with Things: Our Brains, Our Delusions, and the Unmaking of the World: Volume Two: What Then is True? London: Perspective Press, 2021.

Monroe, Robert A. Ultimate Journey. New York: Harmony Books, 1994.

Percival, Harold Waldwin. Democracy Is Self-Government: The Word Foundation, 1952.

Swann, Ingo. Resurrecting the Mysterious: Ingo Swann's 'Great Lost Work'. Swann-Ryder Productions LLC, 2020.

Valeri, Don. The Origins of Servant Leadership: Servant Leaders Past and Potential Future. LAP Lambert Academic Publishing, 2011.

Chapter Five

The Ethics And Moral Foundation Of A 5th Dimensional World

The key to growth is the introduction of higher dimensions of consciousness into our awareness, Lao Tzu

Ethics Today: What Ethics?

It is a truism, apparent to anyone with any ethical awareness and a rational, critical mind, that we now live in a most unethical time. It's as if Shakespeare put it correctly when he said, "hell is empty and all the devils are here." The slow demise of the Christian religion in the West has played a role. The Christian churches, not necessarily in complete, wholesome, or healthy ways, provided people with some ethical teachings and had given them a 'manual' to rely on, being Scriptures. In recent decades, church attendances have fallen dramatically, church leaders attacked, and churches burned. Satanic artistic expressions in the movie and music industries have proliferated thanks to the World Wide Web and social media.

Secondly, the rise of communist policies and cultural Marxism in so many Western institutions have contributed to this development. People forget that it was Marx who cynically remarked "religion is the opium of the masses." The god of communism was the state, which was committed to destroying any vestige of religion as well as the family. Its offshoot, Cultural Marxism, has created division, civil war, and mind control using hidden techniques institutionally imposed on us. People are now defined by ephemeral, tertiary, secondary characteristics such as race, gender, or religion, and encouraged to see themselves as oppressed minorities, perpetual victims. Their perceived victimhood permits them to have a revenge impulse that can be used and cultivated against their perceived systemic oppressors, especially white European males. Their enraged acts of violence and destruction are, therefore, justified and moral. The Old Testament morality of 'an eye for an eye' has returned with a vengeance.

There is a third development that has insidiously contributed to this unethical age, and that is the replacement of a non-corporeal god with a technocratic one. Technology has now become many people's god whom they unknowingly worship as a religion. There are those who truly believe that technology can solve all our human problems. Some technocrats like Ray Kurzweil actually think that technology will give us immortal life, as he supposedly believes he can transfer his own human consciousness into a computer and download it in the future somehow. Humans in his world will have censors implanted under their skin, mechanical body parts installed to replace their limbs and organs, and will see empathy as a flaw. This is a form of insanity that only a lunatic whose god is a machine could believe. In such a 3D matrix world, there will be machines and no more humans or humanity. Only an age devoid of ethical thinking and behaviour is capable of producing this kind of madness. It is a techno totalitarian world that Canadian futurist Marshall McLuhan foresaw in 1964: "After three thousand years of explosion, by means of fragmentary and mechanical technologies, the Western world is imploding. During the mechanical age, we had extended our bodies in space. Today, after more than a century of electric technology, we have extended our central nervous system itself in a global embrace, abolishing both space and time as far as our planet is concerned. Rapidly, we approach the final phase of the extension of man –the technological simulation of consciousness, when the creative process of knowing will be collectively and corporately extended to the whole of human society, much as we have already extended our senses and nerves by various media. Whether the extension of consciousness, so long sought by advertisers for specific products, will be "a good thing" is a question that admits of a wide solution."[1]

A New Paradigm of Ethics

The troubling question posed here is whether there can ever be an evolution of human consciousness. If not, then all human life is in jeopardy. But if so, then humanity has a bright and brilliant future. But when and how long will it take? No matter how and when it unfolds, it will have a moral and ethical foundation. We can look at the ancient laws reflected in the Code of Hammurabi, the Ten Commandments, the 12 Tables of Roman law, Marcus Aurelius' Meditations, and many other sources for guidance. Many of those laws will still apply. No society can exist very long without a moral base and the rule of law. In a 5D world, however, there will be other characteristics such as the following, which in many ways will supersede these ancient laws:

1. It will be wrong to lie, steal, cheat, or defraud someone, and everyone will instinctively know this.
2. Infringing on another person or their property will be wrong.
3. People will be able to distinguish between human envy and jealousy. The former occurs when we see someone with something we would like to have or experience. This is normal. Jealousy refers to this feeling, but it turns into actions and thoughts that seek to destroy what that other person is or has that we would like to be or have. You believe that since you cannot

---

[1] Eric McLuhan, Frank Zingrone, Editors, Essential McLuhan (Concord Ontario, Anansi Press, 1995), p. 149.

have it, then similarly, no one else can. This is clearly an evil and destructive human trait that must be expunged.

4. That which is human will be superior to that which is technological. Machines will be subservient to humans. The efficiency and speed of machines must not be allowed to exist at the expense of human emotion, of losing our ability to feel empathy, sympathy, or compassion for another being or animal. The idea that we can do better without nature will be seen as preposterous and insane.

5. People will have the right to acquire property, but not an unlimited license to acquire so much property that they limit and restrain others from having property. People can create as much abundance as it is possible for them, provided they do not rob other people's wealth to do so.

6. The crime of ecocide will be the law in every country. Nature and all animal, insect, plant, and fish life will be respected, protected, and cherished. Being able to connect with nature will be the supreme virtue.

7. Conflicts will be resolved peacefully and never end in acts of violence.

8. All forms of slavery, whether human or digital, will be abolished.

9. The right to privacy will be maintained, and no one or institution will have the right to spy or surveil other humans without their express permission.

10. The caring for and educating of children will be the highest calling and priority in a human family. Children will be encouraged to seek out and express their talents and the gifts they were born with.

11. Everyone will have the right to adequate housing and medical care of their choosing.

12. When in doubt, the Golden Rule shall apply. All actions shall be governed by the fundamental principle of "do no harm" to another human or sentient being (primum non nocere).

Just about all of the characteristics listed here, which are plain and simple to understand, even by a child, are reflections of higher values that will come to fruition in a 5D world. Unfortunately, implementing them and applying them in today's 3D world is what is so challenging for humans. Making them come alive will require an extension and metamorphous of human consciousness, which will bring about a true evolution of human morality.

The Shift in Consciousness and Its Ethical Implications

From today's perspective, however, these 5D characteristics seem not only surrealistic, but a fantasy. But there is increasing hope that humans with a higher level of consciousness, with enhanced consciences, could make these values common, even the norm. Though not easy to see, human consciousness has already begun to shift. People are no longer willing to go to war, especially another world war, which could end all life on the planet. There is growing intolerance for the levels of poverty, extremes of wealth, the corruption of disingenuous political rulers, the degradation and destruction of nature, the phony news and propaganda media, an educational system that seeks to indoctrinate and misinform, a judicial system that has little to do with justice and a medical system run by large pharmaceutical companies that cause more illness than health. The awareness of all these social ills is spreading, in spite of all the draconian and totalitarian measures through which governments seek to preserve them and the steps they take to thwart and dismiss their critics. To be a dissenter or dissident is to risk not only ostracism but prosecution in many states. Yet more people are bravely stepping forward in spite of the harm and suffering they incur. Whether they know it or not, in their hearts, they believe that the world the Nazarene spoke of in his Sermon on the Mount will someday come to pass.

To contemplate an evolution in morality, it might be useful to consider the growth and development of a child. When born, an innocent child does not have a moral compass. Gradually, it learns that if it hurts another, takes from another without permission, or lies that there will be repercussions. Eventually, it will have feelings of guilt and shame, which it was not born with, and can have unhealthy effects if used to manipulate someone, but can also serve as internal signals that you may have caused harm to someone. These are acquired habits of being human that parents and teachers instill in the child by giving or withholding love and acceptance. In other words, one gradually develops a conscience and becomes cognizant of the effects of his or her behaviour on others. One might even develop the ability, and this is rare, to see oneself as others see you. Modern civilization has made normal life so complicated and complex it is very difficult now for a human to foresee all the possible consequences of one's behaviour. Moral development itself is a long process and may not be complete until the child is in early adulthood. Unlike other animals, we do not emerge from the wombs of our mothers as fully developed humans. The gestation period and growth time for a human from childhood to adulthood is one of the longest in nature. This is the nature of our 3D world today.

Now, suppose human consciousness evolved somehow more quickly such that the gestation and childhood growth and development no longer required 25 or more years to reach a mature adulthood, mentally and morally. Imagine how much human behaviour would change as we moved into a 5D world. The moral behaviour of a young teenager would be the equivalent of mature adult. They would instinctively know the difference between right and wrong, need far less control and supervision, and not have to slowly learn all the hard lessons teenagers must now do. Human brains would be left and right hemispheres balanced. Suppose also that humans had the ability to pick up precognitively what another person was thinking telepathically, the way some mammals do, like dolphins and whales, who also have the largest brains amongst the mammal species. What is intriguing is that we might also be able to intuit whether people are telling the truth by reading their auras. The only potential downside to this might be the reduction in time spent in a "play-based childhood" through which children learn social skills, learn from mistakes, acquire feedback from playmates, read other children's feelings, resolve conflicts, and grow emotionally.[2] Hopefully, this time will not be replaced with more of the silicon "phone-based reality" that so many children experience today.

Social scientists, like Timothy R. Levine, have pointed out that humans now have a "truth default" mental mechanism. We uncritically, as a general rule, accept most of the messages we receive as "honest". In other words, we are hard-wired to being deceived. This vulnerability to deception erodes our trust in other people and social institutions. Speaking of levels of consciousness, David R. Hawkins has opined that the only thing that brings about any restraint in today's world is the law itself. The reason we didn't lie to each other is because we relied upon each other. In today's world, it is a threat of a lawsuit.[3] Obviously, there are many situations in which people instinctively disbelieve what someone is telling them. It could be because we have caught the person previously lying, or we know that, being a politician or used car salesperson, we would be foolish to rely on their word. But without a "truth default" mechanism, humans would question and disbelieve everything they are told, and this would bring human interaction to a halt. One would have to fact-check and cross-examine everything one is told, an exhausting, time-consuming activity that would never end. Everything said to us would have to be filtered through a lie detector device. No one would trust anyone.

---

[2] Jonathan Haidt, <u>The Anxious Generation</u> (New York, Penquin, 2024), pp.52-54.
[3] David R. Hawkins, <u>In the World, but not of it</u> (Carlsbad, CA, Hay House, 2023), p. 61.

There are a number of hidden benefits with this increase in human sensitivity with higher consciousness. We will no longer have to rely on lie detectors. Courtroom trials will no longer take days of cross-examination to test the veracity of witnesses. Governments and politicians will have to tell people the truth, which is hard to imagine right now. Human relations will improve as people learn there is no advantage to lying. It is even possible that this consciousness will extend to the lying we do to ourselves. We often have no idea how much lying we do to ourselves, but this human frailty may recede in the damage it causes. Lying is one of the prime traits of a psychopath. It will now be possible to easily spot the psychopath by the level and magnitude of deception they carry out. What kind of world will it be when we no longer have to worry about a psychopath as a 'ruler' or corporate executive? Psychopaths will be shunned and ostracized and no longer considered for 'leadership' or management roles.

Some Economic Consequences for a 3D World

Even more uplifting will be the change in ethos of our business and economic 'managers' who predominate in the marketplace. It is no exaggeration to say that the business model of so many companies today is based on fraud. This will change, facilitated by the collapse and bankruptcy of so many of these fraudulent enterprises, as the planet transitions from 3D and 4D to 5D. It is evident today that the benefits of the capitalist system have been perverted and transformed into what is known as "crony capitalism," buttressed by financial capitalist economic systems throughout much of the planet. The central and chief advantage of the capitalist system is that the output that is created is more valuable than the resources that go into creating it. The result is a more efficient capital market that facilitates savings and provides capital resources to those who can best combine them with their ideas and convert them into profits and productivities that raise living standards. This is how capitalism is supposed to work. Unfortunately, countries plagued by poor education, a poor culture that impedes people from working together effectively, poor infrastructure, and, most sadly, too much debt, together cause bad economic results. Moreover, those with wealth and power seek to 'game' the system to their own advantage. One method is to externalize the costs of their businesses, like the pollution that they cause, and pass them on to consumers or the government. In other words, the supposed advantage of market capitalism in setting fair prices is based on a false premise. It is incapable of recognizing and reflecting the true costs of products and services. Another game played is to transfer capital assets from the balance sheet to the income ledger, an accounting mechanism that portrays business organizations as profitable when they can actually be losing money. It is also a method of transferring resources used by one generation, which compromises the ability of future generations to fulfill similar needs. In short, we have a marketplace that is immune to community accountability, and corporate fascists who seek to perpetuate it by rigging and controlling the political and legal systems. An American, Paul Hawken, has summarized this situation as follows:

> We have a long tradition in this country of arguing for the cheapest price for everything, decrying any regulation or law that would inflate prices as being punitive to the little guy. Like many political axioms, the truth is probably the opposite. By arguing for cheapness, we may have dampened invention, innovation, and job creation while at the same time strengthening large corporations, the concentration of wealth, and the disenfranchisement of the poor. Because pricing and costs are divorced in the marketplace, we have an economy in which businesses that are more efficient

than their competitors are unable to compete with less worthy enterprises that externalize their costs.[4]

Another unethical feature of the marketplace is the role played by advertising and marketing.

The concept of 'truth in advertising' is a myth. Thanks to the work of Edward Bernays, Sigmund Freud's nephew and the father of public relations, using mass psychology and other social sciences, people could be persuaded and influenced unconsciously. Taping into a person's unconscious could then be used to persuade someone to buy all kinds of products and services that they don't really need, but bring subconscious satisfaction. How many homes, cars, shoes, or toys does one need to be happy or content? Human wants can become insatiable. What is sad is that so many people are deceived by this process. They are spiritually empty, and the only thing that curtails them seems to be a lack of money. In a 5D world, people will be far less gullible. Knowing better what their true long-term needs are, they will not be so easily conned or persuaded. Having greater access to their higher selves will make this a reality. It is important to realize that by 'dimension', one is referring to our mental and etheric awareness, a state of consciousness, not a physical reality. In a 5D world, human vibrations are much lighter and faster, less dense than in the 3D world, which makes this possible. This will be preceded by a flowering of esoteric knowledge and wisdom. Teachers and leaders will emerge who will help people through meditation, prayer, breath work, and plant medicines to experience their inner luminosity. They will know that so many of the simple things in life, like friendship, love, family, and living in harmony with nature, are the true cornerstones of wealth.

---

[4] Paul Hawken, <u>The Ecology of Commerce, Revised Edition</u> (New York, Harper Business, 2010), p.99.

The decadence and malfeasance of the marketplace have never perhaps, been apparent than with the way Wall Street bankers and investors were treated during and after the 2008 financial meltdown. Every major bank in the U.S. was technically bankrupt. Millions of people lost their homes. Yet no one at the top of these banks or financial institutions went to jail for fraud. Shockingly, they made sure they got their annual bonuses after nearly sinking their ships. Equally egregious are the findings of Dr. Mark Skidmore, an academic from Michigan State University, showing that over $21 trillion has been stolen from the U.S. government and its agencies. Yet no one seems to be looking for it. And since he made his findings public, that number has grown even larger. So, it is arguable that these banks and the U.S. government are now nothing more than criminal enterprises. They will not survive the transition to a 5D world in their present form.

Religious and Political 5D Implications

Lastly, a few words concerning our current political and religious institutions need to be made since they play such a large role in shaping human morality. Our current technological development has clearly advanced more rapidly than the natural evolution of our emotional and moral conditions. Our political and religious institutions have not addressed this development, and are therefore a central part of the problem. Politically, the movement towards greater control and centralization of power is doomed to accelerate this process. Only a decentralization of power and authority can arrest this so that people can take greater control and responsibility for what they and their children will experience. The mind-controlled and controlling oligarchs are doing everything they can to prevent this. Deep down, they know that this will be a revolution, an end to their reign, for it will be an expression of ideas whose time has finally come, to paraphrase Victor Hugo.

As to religions, they too will change in order to survive in a 5D world. They will have to divest themselves of hierarchical structures, join together in dialogue, and though they may be unique, they will all express the same compassionate purpose. They will see that it is fine to worship as you wish, and simultaneously acknowledge the right of others to worship as they see fit. This will be part of an expansion of the planet's spiritual awareness from increased knowledge, wisdom, understanding, and compassion. The doctrinal separation and radicalism of today, which have led to theocratic dictatorships, will be seen as lower consciousness and not of God.[5] It will be a world based on generosity, magnanimity, and morality, not division, hatred, pettiness, meanness, and obsession with power over others.

An Example of 3D to 5D Ethical Awareness

There is undoubtedly a wide chasm between a 3D ethical world and a 5D one. How can this gap possibly be bridged? Perhaps a story illustrates how. There is a Biblical story from the New Testament, the Book of John (8:3 - 11). The Pharisees and scribes brought a woman guilty of adultery to Jesus and asked him what he thought they should do. The law then demanded that she be stoned to death. Actually, the Pharisees were trying to trick Jesus and expose him for contradicting himself. On the one hand, Jesus had claimed he had come to fulfill the law, which logically meant go ahead and stone her. But Jesus had also preached forgiveness and mercy, and he would therefore say, let her go. Either way, the Pharisees could expose and criticize Jesus as a hypocrite. This is a good example of 3D thinking and values; logical, dogmatic, fear and revenge-based, even the end justifying the means. Jesus responds by not falling

----

[5] Monika Muranyi, The Human Soul Revealed (Outremont, Quebec Ariane, 2015), pp.204-204.

into their trap. He picks up a stone like them and says, "Let him who is without sin cast the first stone." What Jesus was saying was that love and compassion, 5D values, were the true and correct ones. Being and living at a 5D consciousness, Jesus demonstrated that he and they did not have to live in a restricted 3D world. The Pharisees and scribes dropped their stones. They were obviously shamed for who amongst them could say he was without sin. In short, Jesus, by his words and actions, based on love and forgiveness, had raised the consciousness of those gathered from a 3D to a 5D level. If we look closely, with courage, there are possibilities of this kind of lifting of consciousness all around us every day.

REFERENCES

Haidt, Jonathan. The Anxious Generation. New York: Penguin, 2024.

Hawken. The Ecology of Commerce, Revised. New York: Harper Business, 2010.

Hawkins, David R. In the World, But Not of It. Carlsbad, CA, Hay House, 2023.

McLuhan, Frank Zingrone, Editors. Essential McLuhan. Concord, Ontario, Aransi Press,1995.

Muranyi, Monika. The Human Soul Revealed. Outremont, Quebec, Ariane, 2015.

CHAPTER SIX

A Lesson From The Past: Have We Been Here Before?

Through that particular period of experiences in Atlantis, the children of the Law of One...were giving period to the concentration of thought for the use of universal forces, through the guidance or direction of the saints (as would be termed today). There are few terms in the present that would indicate the state of consciousness; save that, through the concentration of the group mind of the children of the Law of One, they entered into a fourth-dimensional consciousness—or were absent from the body. Edgar Cayce reading from "Edgar Cayce on Atlantis" pp 102-103.

Spiritual Dimensions:

There is a growing awareness that the current paradigm of values is eroding, if not collapsing in slow motion. Humanity is becoming aware that it is entrapped in an information cage, enforced by a cybernetic web. Every action and thought is monitored and influenced. Constant surveillance and data manipulation prevail in the most technologically and economically advanced countries. Gradually, more and more people are becoming aware and are yearning for freedom and for ways to break the chains of this information prison. To obtain this freedom, humans will first have to experience a revelation that awakens them to the entrapment that confines them. Whether this will happen in the near or distant future is unknown from today's perspective. A change in consciousness by necessity will precede it. And how that will occur is currently not clear. Another question is, has this higher level of consciousness ever occurred before in human history? Is there a precedent for believing it is possible?

The concept of the fifth dimension has certain philosophical and metaphysical implications. It challenges our traditional notions of reality about the nature of existence and consciousness. Could there be higher dimensions of reality that we are unaware of, where reality is fundamentally different from our perception? Could there even be beings or civilizations that exist in dimensions beyond our current comprehension?

One method to approach these questions is to look at language and etymology. We use words to express our ideas and thoughts. Without words, mental processes cannot occur, and thoughts could not be said to exist. Since thinking, conscious or not, precedes all actions. Understanding the language and words that humans use is essential to understanding human behaviour. We could start with the word "consciousness" and look at it the way Ingo Swann did:

> The other mode is one in which history is viewed as an archaeological situation – a problem and archaeology in which physical and linguistic artifacts are rediscovered or encountered that no longer fit into history nor are explainable by history alone. The ancient Sanskrit, Hebrew, Tibetan, and Chinese languages (to name only a few) are littered with linguistic artifacts that do establish that in the distant past, there were cultures that knew of high consciousness states since their languages had words for those states. The more recent Western European languages (English, German, French, Italian, etc) do not contain words for

these states – and we are thus somewhat culturally inferior insofar as direct knowledge of them is concerned.[1]

What Ingo Swann is suggesting here is that certain societies had developed language, words, and concepts that referred to "consciousness." Other societies, like modern Western European languages, did not, or could not, because the concept was not part of thinking and nor culturally expressed. In the former, consciousness awareness was a fabric of their culture. In the latter, such awareness appears possible, though it may have persisted or evolved in secret societies, religious institutions, or other non-mainstream organizations. It is also possible that in ancient societies that relied on Sanskrit, Hebrew, Tibetan, or Chinese, that it may have only existed or been preserved in the priestly castes, and not widely known among the greater populace. Yet, the possibility that it could spread to the population as a whole was there.

An analogy here can be drawn in the social revolution and the birth of New Age thinking since World War Two. The influence from the East, from the work of philosophers and sages like Krishnamurti, Yogananda, Vivekananda, the Zen Masters, and many others, found fertile soil in the West to take root in. Had they come before this modern time, they may not have bloomed, despite the work of a few enlightened souls and the more or less hidden mystery schools. Two important developments are now evident and plain to see: 1) An expansion of human consciousness is now unfolding, and 2) the growing awareness that humanity is ruled by pyramid structures dominated by psychopathic elites at the pinnacle. Both of these developments and revelations are leading to what some have called the "Great Awakening."

A Previous 5D Civilization?

---

[1] Ingo Swann, Resurrecting the Mysterious: Ingo Swann's Great Last Work (Swann-Ryder Productions, 2020), p.266.

One profound and serious question that one has to ponder is, has there ever been a 5D civilization in human history? If so, could we not look to it to see how such a civilization came to be or evolved into its higher evolution? Looking at the vast panoply of human civilization in the last 6,000 to 7,000 years, or what is commonly referred to as 'recorded' history, the answer is clearly no. Yes, there have been highly theocratic, religious, or priestly run societies, but they do not qualify as a 5D civilization as has been defined here. Such a civilization would be one in which a consciousness of compassion, light, freedom, and universal love prevailed. Yet, when taking an archaeological and linguistic approach, one can see some clues of possible societies that approached the 5D dimension. There are physical and linguistic artifacts rediscovered or encountered which no longer fit the conventional or academic explanation of how history has unfolded. Some will be discussed in this chapter.

Recorded or written history of the last 7000 years fails to show any such utopian state. Is there a possibility during the pre-deluvian history that such a society might have developed? The end of the Younger Dryas period, which was an extinction-level event, ended in the great floods and the permanent inundation of vast portions of land that wiped out many highly advanced human cities and societies. This event was expressed in many mythologies, religious scriptures, esoteric writings, and ancient oral stories and traditions passed on by indigenous peoples in Australia and the Americas. There is one story, though, that is particularly compelling. That is the story told by Plato of the Atlantis civilization in his writings *Critias* and *Timaeus.* It is compelling and cited by many scholars, historians, and philosophers. It tells the story of a very advanced technological civilization that rose and met a catastrophic end. Many others have spoken of the Atlantis mythology: Diodorus Siculus, Rudolf Steiner, Helen Blavatsky, Edgerton Sykes, Lewis

Spence, Ignatius Donnelly, Otto Muck, and Edgar Cayce, and numerous channelers. Plato's description is revealing:

> Now, this was the power, so great and so extraordinary, that existed in that distant region at that time. This was the power the god mustered and brought against these [Mediterranean] lands. It was said that his pretense was something like what I shall describe. For many generations and as long as enough of her divine nature survived, they were obedient unto their laws, and they were well disposed to the divinity they were kin to. They possessed conceptions that were true and entirely lofty. And in their attitude to the disasters and chance events that constantly befall men and their relations with one another, they exhibited a combination of mildness and prudence, because, except for virtue, they held all else in disdain and thought of their present good fortune of no consequence. They bore their vast wealth of gold and other possessions without difficulty, treating them as if they were a burden. They did not become intoxicated with the luxury of the life their wealth made possible; they did not lose their self-control and slip into decline, but in their sober judgment, they could see distinctly that even their very wealth increased with their amity and its companion, virtue. But they saw that both wealth and concord decline as possessions become pursued and honored. And virtue perishes with them as well.
>
> Now, because these were their thoughts and because of the divine nature that survived in them, they prospered greatly as we have already related. But when the divine portion in them began to grow faint as it was often blended with great checkers of morality and as their human nature gradually gained ascendancy, at that moment, in their inability to bear their good fortune, they became disordered. To whoever had eyes to see, they appeared hideous, since they were losing the finest of what were once their most treasured possessions. But to those who were blind to see the true way oriented to happiness, it was at this time that they gave the

semblance of being supremely beauteous and blessed. Yet inwardly they were filled with an unjust lust for possessions and power. But as Zeus, god of gods, reigning as king according to law, could clearly see this state of affairs, he observed this noble race lying in this abject state and resolved to punish them and to make them more careful and harmonious as a result of their chastisement...[2]

Whether Atlantis ever existed or is just a fable or myth is a question that may never be answered conclusively, and can be set aside momentarily. When one looks closely at Plato's language, Atlantis was a truly unique civilization that had achieved a very high level of development and a high standard of living for its people. This was not a primitive hunter-gatherer civilization. Some of those who have written about Atlantis believe that they had tapped into nuclear power, and, unknown even today, enormous crystalline power that they had discovered through special and unique crystals. They were able to develop flying aircraft, even spacecraft. And all of these incredible achievements were done some 20,000 years ago, a time that modern anthropologists believe Cro Magnon humans lived in caves.

From a spiritual perspective, when a society arrives at or achieves a high level of prosperity and abundance, it then becomes possible for its people to find and enjoy the leisure time to look inwardly and turn to spiritual development. Without this level of prosperity, the life of the vast majority will be consumed in survival activities, finding shelter, food, protection from predators, and invasive external tribes or peoples. Their lives will be consumed in dreary drudgery at the meanest levels, with little or no time for education, reflection, prayer, or meditation.

----
[2] John M. Cooper, editor, Plato Complete Works (Indianapolis, Indiana, Hackett Publishing Company Inc. 1997), p. 1306.

Only a tiny few would be able to do so, and often did so, becoming the priestly or shaman class from which spiritual teachers or avatars could evolve and emerge. One can see this in many ancient civilizations that existed in the last 6,000 years, including the Sumerian, Babylonian, Chinese, Egyptian, Greek, and Mayan civilizations that emerged from tribal hunter-gather levels of development.

One can find some clarity here if one refers to what German philosopher Karl Jaspers called the Axial Age, which he believed was pivotal to the spiritual development of ancient humanity. From about 900 to 200 BC, in four distinct regions, the great world traditions that continued to assist humanity came into being: Confucianism and Daoism in China, Hinduism and Buddhism in India, monotheism in Israel, and philosophical rationalism in Greece. This is the period when Buddha, Socrates, Confucius, Zoroaster, and Jeremiah, the mystics of the Upanishads, Mencius, and Euripides appeared. Spiritually, this was a period of intense creativity, and spiritual and philosophical geniuses opened human minds and pioneered an entirely new kind of human experience. In the opinion of Karen Armstrong, "the Axial Age was one of the most seminal periods of intellectual, psychological, philosophical, and religious change in recorded history." There would be nothing comparable to it until the Great Western Transformation, which created our own scientific and technological modernity.[3]

The most pressing question arising from the myth or fable of Atlantis is whether there are any spiritual lessons one can learn from it that applies to our present age. There is the story of God's punishment for a wayward and corrupt people, with Zeus' chastisement. Similar explanations prevailed with the Great Flood that Noah survived or God's punishment of the people of Babylon

---

[3] Karen Armstrong, The Great Transformation: The Beginning of our Religious Tranditions (Alfred A. Knopf, New York, 2006), p.xii.

for their arrogance in building the Tower of Babel. With our current technological prowess and the dangers posed by nuclear weapons, there is an ominous sense of forebodement when one hears how the Atlanteans destroyed themselves. So, as humans, we should ask have we been here before?

The language of Plato is revealing. He speaks of the "divine nature" which continued as long as they were "obedient unto their laws and well-disposed to the divinity they were kin to." This clearly indicates that the Atlanteans possessed a spiritual appreciation and disposition. Plato also points to the highly prized virtuous nature of the Atlanteans. They valued virtue more highly than "gold and other possessions," which they saw as "burdens". Their abundance came from their highly developed spirituality: 'because of the divine nature that survived in them, they prospered greatly.' Plato claims that Atlantis' decline was directly related to the evaporation of the "divine portion in them" as they became filled with an unjust lust for possessions and power." As a result, they incurred the wrath of Zeus and were suitably punished. One can see many parallels on the planet today.

Plato relates the history and geography of Atlantis in great detail. He speaks very little, however, of how the Atlantean civilization was ruled and governed, except to say that it was divided into ten districts, each ruled by a king, who passed his kingship onto his eldest son. There are, however, stories of the Atlanteans' enslavement of people and committing genetic mutations and manipulations, and using their advanced technologies to conquer land and other peoples. One will never know how accurate these stories are, but their resemblances to modern states and imperial developments of the last several thousand years of human activity are noteworthy.

Recent studies of the pyramids and the great sphinx in Egypt have indicated that they may have been built thousands of years before the Egyptian pharaohs by a pre-diluvian civilization. It is speculated that the pyramids were used as communication and energy sources, possibly using scalar wave technology that Nikola Tesla discovered or rediscovered. Pyramids were built all over the planet by various civilizations, notably in Mexico and China, leading to the possibility of a worldwide spread of this technology. Unfortunately, the Atlanteans' obsession with power, wealth, and their abuse of these technologies contributed to their demise. It is also believed that the Atlanteans were eventually afflicted by black magic arts, including necromancy, dark occultism, and the diabolical crafts of sorcerers that debased their previous divine esoteric and mystical higher evolution.

Atlantis is not the only ancient civilization that had discovered advanced technologies. The Hindu Mahabharata, Vedas, and Sanskrit texts speak of this and their flying aircraft, Vimanas. It appears possible that this ancient Indian civilization coexisted with Atlantis, possibly some 15,000 years ago. According to the texts, it also perished in a nuclear holocaust, suggesting that it, too, like the Atlanteans, had discovered how to split the atom and release incredible energy. We currently believe that this discovery did not occur until the twentieth century.

Since the focus of this book is leadership, or more precisely, leaders, it is necessary to speculate and try to ascertain what type of leaders prevailed in these prediluvian ancient civilizations. Again, it may be more accurate to refer to them as 'rulers'. According to Plato, Atlantis was divided into a number of "kingdoms". Each of the kings of Atlantis had complete control over his own kingdom, and their mutual relationships were governed by a code engraved by the first ten kings on a column of precious orichalcum standing in a temple in the city of Poseidon. The chief laws of the kingdoms were that they should not take up arms against each other, and that they should come to the assistance of any of them who is attacked. In matters of war and great significance, the final decisions were in the hands of the descendants of the family of Atlas. No king had the power of life and death over his people without the assent of a majority of the ten kingdoms.[4]

One can only speculate, using a similar recorded history of 'kingdoms' in the last several thousand years, that after a sufficient number of generations, these ten Atlantean kingdoms had gradually become primarily oligarchic in structure. By oligarchic is meant rule by the few, especially for corrupt and selfish purposes. It does not seem likely that these were democratic societies, or ones in which those who governed only did so with the consent of the governed, or a majority of the governed. As in so much human history, there were rulers and the ruled. For many years, possibly thousands in Atlantis, the ruled were placated and kept satisfied by the abundance that the Atlantean civilization had created through their mastery of technology and the forces of nature. Their ethical and moral balance, and spiritual advancement, which Plato points out, contributed immensely to the preservation of a peaceful, happy, and generous society. It is nonetheless difficult to see it as a 5D civilization, and if it was, for how long?

To discover how much of a 5D civilization Atlantis may have been, one must look to see how it was governed. Plato does not make it very clear how Atlantis was governed, except to talk about "kingdoms" or monarchies ruled ultimately by "kings". One can only speculate here. Whether you take his writings as mythical, historical, or allegorical, some preliminary conclusions can be drawn, even though one is imagining a society from a 21st-century perspective and is vulnerable to the criticism of

----
[4] Manly Palmer Hall, The Secret Teachings of All Ages (New York, Discovery Publisher, 2020), pp. 60-62.

presentism. One can still focus on 'leadership' or 'rulership' as an expression of the human experience, even when one looks at this ancient civilization.

It is almost a truism, if not a historical fact, that monarchies have existed unabetted for thousands of years of recorded history. It may even be the most common form of "rulership" developed by humans. Starting with the French Revolution and finishing with World War I in the 20th century, this form of rulership met its demise and no longer commands the reverence it once had. The question is, why did it survive for so long? Why did it take revolutions and world wars to cause its collapse? Few if any want to see its return. According to Plato, though, it survived for thousands of years in Atlantis. How or why?

Monarchies offer the image or perception of stability, as opposed to a crowd. There is no upheaval, usually, when the monarch dies. The throne passes on to the next of kin, a blood or family relative. The rule is determined by hereditary status. Aristotle considered a virtuous monarch who rules for the common good a blessed state. He was not a fan of democracies. In a democracy, by contrast, power passes to a different set of "rulers" who can or will bring disturbing and unsettling changes to the way, "things are done." This can be threatening to those who have benefitted most from their allegiance and closeness to the monarch. Will they lose their power, positions, prestige, property, and privileges? What will happen to their children and families?

Secondly, monarchies offer a very convenient form and expression of centralized power. Centralized power makes it easier to maintain control and efficiency, extend power, disrupt dissent, and stymie changes that the ruling class or monarchy does not wish to see. Conversely, absolute power, as Lord Acton put it, corrupts absolutely. It can even degenerate into a ruthless tyranny. Such power is very difficult to resist, oppose, or overthrow. It is tailor-made for societies that are built and thrive on slavery, though slavery has also existed from time to time in oligarchic, republican, and democratic societies, such as ancient Athens, Rome, and the U.S., before it was abolished as a result of a catastrophic, bloody, and costly civil war.

Thirdly, monarchies prey on human weakness, laziness, and vulnerability. Unlike a true and vibrant democracy, the ordinary person has no responsibility for governing. This is one reason why one is called a "subject" and not a "citizen" in monarchical societies. The individual can sit back and let others do the heavy lifting, make the tough decisions and choices, and take the blame when things work out poorly. Humans are prone to surrender a lot of personal freedom for the chimera of security. Most of the time, they end up with neither.

Fourthly, the practice of governing, when other people are involved, is messy, complicated, and costly. It requires humans to be governed by their "better" angels, as Abraham Lincoln might have put it. How many monarchs are kind, loving, and wise? Plato had a lot of prescient and profound thoughts concerning these issues. In his Republic, he expressed the view that leadership or rulership, as he may have thought of it, would best be expressed when "philosophers were kings or kings and princes of this world have the spirit and power of philosophy, and political greatness and wisdom meet in one."[5] Recorded history has shown this to be exceedingly rare. Thus, one is in awe if Atlantis was able to produce such "rulers" during its long existence.

Such 'rulers' who emerged to produce an advanced 5D civilization were most likely benefiting from the high technology foundation that Atlantis was built on. This included

---

[5] Don Valeri, The Origin of Servant Leadership (Lambert Academic Publishing, 2007), p. 17.

the use of magnetic and antigravity energy, atomic power, genetic engineering, lasers, sonic levitation, and crystal (Tuaoi Stone)/crystalline power were among their supposed scientific achievements according to the Cayce readings.[6] The Atlanteans were able to build canal networks, temples, palaces, bridges, tunnels, elaborate harbors, ships, and even aircraft. It is even believed by some that they were able to make contact with extraterrestrial species who may have helped them in developing technologies for living, leaving them with enough leisure time to explore their spiritual natures. Instead of laboring and exhausting themselves with survival activities, they had time to meditate deeply, pray, read, study, and seek to explore their higher selves and develop spiritual wisdom and powers. They may have developed psychic powers, visualization practices, clairvoyance, clairaudience, clairsentience, precognition, telepathic communication and healing modalities, and other avenues to their multidimensional selves. If built upon a moral foundation, these expressed powers may have truly flowered into a 5th-Dimensional Civilization.

The obvious question here is how such a highly advanced civilization, technologically and spiritually, could collapse. Plato offers one explanation. As their wealth and prosperity increased, so did their greed, ambition, and lust for power and material possessions increase. The population grew, and as land was increasingly lost to the sea, its kings desired more territory and living space to replace the missing land, but never from a neighboring king, but from lands in adjacent continents, in the Americas, Africa, and as far as into the Mediterranean as Egypt and northern Italy. Some of these wars and conquests are referred to by Plato. And as morality disintegrated at home, so it was reflected in the actions of the soldiers of Atlantis. At home, it is believed that a highly centralized socialist form of government prevailed, and the 'state' or kingdom owned all the

---

[6] Shirley Andrews, <u>Atlantis; Insights from a Lost Civilization</u> (St. Paul, Minn., Llewellyn Publications, 2001) p. 159.

lands, industries, systems of public transportation, and communication.[7]

As noted, the favorable living conditions in Atlantis expanded their daily opportunities for leisure and introspective thought. Atlantean priests, seeking an understanding of themselves and the universe, developed their already potent psychic abilities to a degree few have ever attained since. They were far more proficient than the most powerful psychics of our time. Unfortunately, their mystical skills gradually combined religion, magic, and science, and the results were dreadful. They grew adept at experimenting with altered states of consciousness, slowing their brain waves, entering trances, and exploring the spirit world. Slowly, religion was interwoven with magic, and the occult sciences were born. Master astrology, necromancy (communication with the spirits of the dead), alchemy, prophecy, and divination (the use of supernatural powers to foresee the future or discover hidden knowledge), as well as knowledge of ritual symbolism, healing, levitation, clairvoyant communication, all occurred. As time went on, these occult practices degenerated into witchcraft and sorcery.[8] Tampering with the human genome to produce a slave species was even carried out.

Worse, according to Shirley Andrews, was the following: "Around 10,000 BC, the self-centered leaders of Atlantis lost interest in material and scientific progress, and their respect for the ancient knowledge vanished. As these powerful Black Priests dedicated their energies to dangerous occult practices, black magic gradually replaced religion in Atlantis. Some mastered the technique of conjuring spirits, not from the higher realm, but from the lower astral or underworld. At the bidding of

---

[7] Ibid., pp. 87-88, p. 92.
[8] Ibid. pp. 104-107.

the dreadful spirits, those who evoked them performed terrible deeds to gain material wealth and power over the freighted populace. Devilish human sacrifice was one of the horrible results. To avoid the wrath of the powerful gods and the underworld spirits served by the evil men, parents sacrifice their children or cut hearts from fellow humans while they were still living and offered them as gifts to the fearful unknown. People were so terrified of these Black Priests they mindlessly obeyed them, even participating in supervised orgies where human blood was consumed."[9] It is remarkable, if not eerie, that the year 10,000 BC is close to the date attributed to the great floods that wiped out many civilizations, and even referred to in the book of Genesis (6:9), as God's punishment for Man's wickedness. The similar demise of Atlantis that Plato describes at this time fits the narrative almost perfectly.

According to the Cayce readings, decades, possibly centuries before, some Atlanteans could see the writing on the wall and decided to emigrate and find new homes. These were individuals who sought to escape the feuding between the followers of Belial (and their decadence, moral turpitude, and obsessions with the dark arts) and the followers of the Law of One. They were likely more balanced humans in terms of their left and right brains. Some went west, to what is now Peru, the Yucatan, parts of Nevada, and Colorado. Other groups headed east to the Pyrenees and Egypt.[10] Many of their descendants could have survived the great geographic calamities, flooding and volcanoes that apparently destroyed Atlantis.

The value of looking at the myth of Atlantis is to see it as a cautionary tale. When you compare the characteristics of Atlantis to our modern Western world, the similarities are uncanny but disturbing. One can almost sense a feeling of déjà vu. Is our world

---

[9] Ibid. pp. 185-186.

[10] Edgar Evans Cayce, Gail Cayce Schwartzer and Douglas G. Richards, <u>Mysteries of Atlantis Revisited</u> (San Francisco, Harper & Row, 1988), p.42.

headed for the same fate? Think of all the alarming parallels and similarities: technological advances, atomic energy, flying aircraft, gene and DNA manipulation, laser and crystalline forms of energy, human mind control, left brain dominance reflected in their obsession with technology, military expansion and conquests, even possible space exploration, obsession with the black arts, and an undeniable level of elite corruption. It is possible the Atlanteans had actually achieved a 5th-dimensional civilization, but Plato's story of Atlantis tells us that they could not sustain it. In the days to come, if humanity somehow achieves a 5th-dimensional civilization, the fate of Atlantis should forever be on its mind and never forgotten.

REFERENCES

Andrews, Shirley. Atlantis: Insights from a Lost Civilization. St. Paul, Minn.: Llewellyn Publications, 2001.

Andrews, Shirley. Lemuria and Atlantis: Studying the Past to Survive the Future. Woodbury, Minn.: Llewellyn Publications, 2022.

Cayce, Edgar Evans. Edgar Cayce on Atlantic. New York: Grand Central Publishing, 1968.

Cayce, Edgar Evans, Gail Cayce Schwartzer, and Douglas G. Richards. Mysteries of Atlantis Revisited. San Francisco: Harper & Row, 1988.

Cooper, John M., ed. Plato: Complete Works. Indianapolis, Indiana: Hackett Publishing Company, 1997.

Cori, Patricia. Atlantis Rising: The Struggle of Darkness and Light. Berkeley, California: North Atlantic Books, 2001.

Donnelly, Ignatius. Atlantis: The Antediluvian World. Legare Street Press. Reprint of the 1882 original.

Hall, Manly Palmer. The Secret Teachings of All Ages. New York: Discovery Publisher, 2020.

Joseph, Frank. The Lost Civilization of Lemuria. Rochester, Vermont: Bear and Company, 2006.

Muck, Otto. The Secret of Atlantis. New York: Times Books, 1976.

Phylos the Tibetan (Frederick Spence Oliver). A Dweller on Two Planets. Pantianos Classics (first published in 1894).

Scott-Elliot, W. The Story of Atlantis. (First printed 1896). The Lost Lemuria (First printed 1904).

Spence, Lewis. The History of Atlantis. Mineola, New York: Dover Publications, 2003 (originally published 1926).

Spence, Lewis. The Occult Sciences of Atlantis. Ultimatum Editions, 2023 (First published in 1943).

Steiner, Rudolf. Atlantis: The Fate of a Lost Land and it Secret Knowledge. East Sussex: Rudolf Steiner Press, 2001.

Swann, Ingo. Resurrecting the Mysterious. Swann-Ryder Publications, 2020.

Valeri, Don. The Origins of Servant Leadership. Lambert Academic Publishing, 2007.

Chapter Seven

Moral Imagination And Its Importance For Leaders Of The Light

"Imagination Rules the World." Napoleon

Amongst the characteristics that leaders of the light will need and must attain is the ability to exercise moral imagination. But what does that mean? Many ethicists have argued that it is only because of our imaginative capacity that we can experience the sort of empathy required to fully appreciate how our decisions and actions might affect other people. For example, if one were to take someone's wallet off the top of your desk, we would not only know that it was wrong, but we would also, by virtue of our ability to apply our imagination, know how distraught and violated that person would feel being robbed.[1] Adam Smith, the author of *The Wealth of Nations*, explained this human experience eloquently in chapter one of his *Theory of Moral Sentiments*:

> How selfish soever man may be supposed, there are evidently some principles in his nature, which interest him in the fortune of others, and render their happiness necessary to him, though he derives nothing from it except the pleasure of seeing it. Of this kind is pity or compassion, the emotion which we feel for the misery of others, when we either see it, or are made to conceive it

---

[1] Ladkin, Donna. Mastering the Ethical Dimensions of Organizations. Edward Elgar, 2015. p. 82

in a very lively manner. That we often derive sorrow from the sorrow of others is a matter of fact too obvious to require any instances to prove it; for this sentiment, like all the other original passions of human nature, is by no means confined to the virtuous and humane, though they perhaps may feel it with the most exquisite sensibility. The greatest ruffian, most hardened violator of the laws of society, is not altogether without it.

As we have no immediate experience of what other men feel, we can form no idea of the manner in which they are affected, but by conceiving what we ourselves should feel in the like situation. Though our brother is upon the rack, as long as we ourselves are at our ease, our senses will never inform us what he suffers. They never did, and never can, carry us beyond our own person, and it is by the imagination only that we can form any conception of what his sensations are. Neither can that faculty help us to this any other way than by representing to us what would be our own, if we were in his case. It is impressions of our own senses only, not those of his, which our imaginations copy. By the imagination we place ourselves in his situation, we conceive ourselves enduring all the same torments, we enter as it were into his body, and become in some measure the same person with him, and thence form some idea of his sensations, and even feel something which, though weaker in degree, is not altogether unlike them. His agonies, when they are thus brought home to ourselves, when we have thus adopted and made our own, begin at last to affect us, and we then tremble and shudder at the thought of what he feels. For as to be in pain or distress of any kind excites the most excessive sorrow, so to conceive or to imagine that we are in it, excites to some degree the same emotion, in proportion to the vivacity or dullness of the conception.[2]

In another graphic example, Smith describes the general but frequent response of people watching a man die by hanging. In Smith's day, public executions were a common event in

----
[2] Smith, Adam. The Theory of Moral Sentiments. Penguin Books, 2009. pp.13-14.

England. He wrote about a man being hanged and the reaction of people watching it; their bodies were twitching and quivering in sympathy. Note that this does not happen when we see this happening in a movie or on television. But when it happens directly, right in front of you, it is a different experience that touches one on a deeper, emotional, and psychic level. Similar feelings of physical discomfort occur when we see or encounter other people, even animals, that are badly injured or in visible pain.[3] Again, it is much different from watching it on a computer or television screen. Think of how you, as a parent, react and feel when you see your child or loved ones in physical pain and suffering. That too affects people on an emotional and psychic level. One has to ask why or how it is that some people who see and watch these occurrences feel and experience nothing. Could it be that those people are showing signs of psychopathy?

The capacity to develop and display one's moral imagination can also be seen on an intellectual level. As others have pointed out, the human capacity to envision metaphors is crucial to developing a moral imagination. A metaphor is a concept that enables one to understand something in terms of something else. People use metaphors every day to communicate. For example, when one person is described as "brighter than a light bulb" or dumber than a "bucket of manure," they are using metaphors to express thoughts, concepts, and ideas or to embellish, clarify, and expand them. The metaphor makes the thought more easily understood. Another vivid example is not to think of an organization as a "machine," which many do, but as a "garden" or "orchestra." It is through language that we come to know and understand better such value-laden concepts as justice, compassion, integrity, respect, honour, or even love. As the academic philosopher Mark Johnson has pointed out, it is through metaphors that we comprehend the differences and similarities between circumstances, and thereby make a judgment about how to approach

---

[3] Ladkin, p.86.

a specific situation. To make a moral decision, one has to have to have the capacity to comprehend beforehand how your actions might affect others. One can never know another's experiences directly, even if we have experienced such an experience ourselves. We therefore rely on metaphorical thinking to ascertain what is situation is like for the other person.[4] In other words, our moral understanding is deeply metaphorical. Accordingly, if a person lacks the ability to think metaphorically,[5] or whose ability to think metaphorically is impaired or underdeveloped, then such a person cannot make the best or even a proper moral decision in many situations. So do we wish to entrust individuals with the power to make crucial moral decisions, upon which human lives may depend, to someone with a contaminated or impaired capacity to think metaphorically? The answer is obvious.

There is another aspect to this cognitive deficiency that raises its ugly head. According to Donna Ladkin, this is the capacity to go beyond just "imagining" to actually bringing a "caring orientation" to the imaginative process. It means being able to consider the impact of one's actions on others from an "affective" perspective: "What will the felt sense of those affected by particular actions be? From an organizational perspective, a caring imagination would take into account not just the financial impact of a decision, but also the impact it will have on the well-being of staff as well as other internal and external stakeholders."[6]

Amongst the roles played by a caring imagination are creating the possibility for empathy, critical thinking, and critical application. Using one's caring imagination activates the

---

[4] Ibid. p.89.
[5] Johnson, Mark. Moral Imagination: Implications of Cognitive Science for Ethics. University of Chicago Press. 1993, p.33.
[6] Ladkin, p 92.

capacity to speculate what another person's life is like, and thereby animates our moral faculties.[7] The key element here is empathy, sometimes referred to as the ability to vicariously enter the body of another and share another's experience. Another closely related concept is "Einfuhlung," a German term conveying the movement of one individual projecting him or herself into another. As biologist and primatologist Frans de Waal has put it, "we can't feel anything that happens outside ourselves, but by unconsciously merging self and other, the other's experiences echo within us. We feel them as if they're our own." In other words, empathy offers humans a window and "direct access to the foreign self." Anyone who studied the animal kingdom has witnessed this in many other species, especially mammals.[8] Perhaps there is a reason why humans consider dogs man's best friend. There are, in fact, many lessons animals can teach us. On a moonlit field after a battle, Napoleon came upon a dog beside the body of his dead master, licking his face and howling. It was a scene that haunted him for the rest of his life: "This soldier, I realized, must have had friends at home and in his regiment; yet he lay there deserted by all except his dog. I looked on, unmoved, at battles which had decided the future of nations. Tearless, I had given orders which brought death to thousands. Yet here, I was stirred, profoundly stirred, stirred to tears. And by what? By the grief of one dog."

What has been considered so far are first-hand direct experiences of empathy. What happens when our actions and reactions are out of sight or hearing, second-hand, so to speak? We are clearly capable of feeling for others based on our reading and thinking about them, but concern based purely on the imagination lacks the strength, emotion, and urgency absent from the immediate, in-your-face experience. Empathy builds on proximity, similarity,

---

[7] Ibid. p. 93.

[8] De Waal, Frans. The Age of Empathy: Nature's Lessons for a Kinder Society. McClelland and Stewart. 2009. p.65.

and familiarity, which is entirely logical given that it likely evolved to promote and sustain group cooperation.[9] In such cases, only one's capacity for moral imagination can influence one's behaviour. Think of how easy it is for modern technocratic soldiers operating a drone from another continent to wipe out an entire village with a click of a mouse on a computer. To the soldier, it is just another video game, only this game kills real people, many of whom are just "collateral damage." Or for billionaire hedge fund managers to eviscerate a company or a country's economy with a mere click or stroke of a computer program that allows massive short selling. Or think of the unspeakable crimes committed by the commissars of the Soviet Union under Joseph Stalin, all of course justified and in the name of the glorious communist dictatorship. With each of these examples, one's inability to imagine morally the devastating consequences of your actions is tantamount to moral bankruptcy. A fortiori, if the people controlling the levers of power or pushing the buttons are psychopaths or sociopaths, who cannot feel real empathy and compassion, one should not be surprised by the horrific, immoral, destructive decisions being made.

There is also a danger here of becoming too obsessed with consequences. If you become too obsessed with them, you can become paralyzed by fear (aka false expectations appearing real) that will prevent you from doing what is right in certain situations. In other words, if you think only or primarily in terms of consequences, you will always find something to keep you stuck, which is often just fear of change. To go through this fear takes a level of courage and imaginative consciousness that can lead to profound and magnificent changes for the better. Not all leaders possess this important faculty.

---

[9] Ibid. p. 221.

Another avenue to understanding moral imagination is to consider how "systems thinking" affects one's capacity to make a moral decision. The system's thinking orientation encourages people to take into account the wider "system" in which any actions or decisions are made. Systems are comprised of interdependent elements, subsystems, networks of relationships, and patterns of interaction. Few systems are linear or sequential in operation. Fewer still are closed. That is, moral systems draw from the environment and emit waste products into it. Naturally, these systems introduce a great deal of complexity when it comes to deciding what is right or wrong in a given situation. There are times when the desire to do good or act ethically can actually cause more destruction than is good, especially within a system not deeply understood. It is crucial, then, to know ahead of time the history, the interrelationships, traditions, imagery, and the deeply held knowledge within the system with which one is trying to influence.[10] One's ability to imagine morally can assist greatly here. Without this ability, one is very likely to run into the law of unintended consequences. In business, these are what moral observers refer to as "external costs," which producers never pay for and leave others with the tab (environmental and habitat destruction, pollution that causes human deaths and health injury, extremes of wealth and poverty that exacerbate social tension and unrest, etc.). There are many examples, however, where nature is successful in converting plant and animal "waste" into environmentally and sustainably end purposes. The current western economic models do not appreciate or value them in their "system's" thinking, so many an immoral decision is never seen for what it is. If one cannot put a dollar sign on it, signifying a profit, it does not exist. In other words, it is the system itself, being imperfect and flawed, which can cause the problem. Many who cannot morally imagine or think outside the box will fail to see this and fall into a

---

[10] Ladkin, pp. 94-95.

pernicious trap. This flaw is sometimes referred to as a failure to think critically.

Another defect in human ethical decision-making is not fully understanding how a "system" can react and interfere with moral thinking. The desire to do good and to act ethically within a "system" not deeply understood can cause more trouble than good. As the saying goes, the road to hell is paved with good intentions. Systems are abstractions; they are not live human beings with a conscience. They cannot feel empathy or compassion. Only the human actors in charge of the system can do that. So, it is imperative that one is able to consider how things might look different from another stakeholder's perspective.[11] It must also be recognized that one can never know all the impacts of any particular decision taken. This is where one's imagination faculties play a crucial role, especially in seeing and revealing the ethical dimensions that otherwise remain obscured.[12] With multiple players and organizations all having a role and intermixing, this process can obviously get very murky and complicated. It is easy in such cloudy atmospheres for the ends to justify the means and for people to only see what suits their personal agenda. Moreover, when the helm is in the hands of psychopaths, whose moral imaginations are obstructed, impaired, or nonexistent, one can only hope that the results will not be catastrophic. As has been argued by the writer, only by eliminating and removing psychopaths from the corridors of power will this ever be possible.

Conclusion

Our imaginative capabilities allow us to "transcend" the distance between our reality and that of others. Recall the words of Napoleon, that imagination rules the world. He also made the

---

[11] Ibid. pp95-96.
[12] Ibid. p.96.

bold statement that "impossible is a word to be found in the dictionary of fools." Given his life and what he accomplished, this was a prophetic observation. One wonders what he thought about the impossible after the Grande Army's disastrous retreat out of Russia. The point here is that our imagination can create a mental reality, a fantasy or dream, that we do not have the energy to actualize. The results can profoundly shake us as the imaginary future turns into a nightmare. On the other hand, moral imagination can overcome cultural influences and conditioning that curtail and limit our freedoms. It can acquaint us with possibilities beyond those that our culture provides. It can enlarge the scope of our desires. It also makes it possible to reflect critically on the culturally given possibilities by comparing and contrasting them with the possibilities we derive from history, ethnography, literature, and our spiritual awareness. It can, in short, increase our freedoms.[13]

The writing here has dealt with how our moral imagination, if not healthy and grounded, can lead us into folly and disaster. But if properly developed, it allows us to perceive how others affect what they see and how they perceive reality. Mark Johnson has defined moral imagination as "an ability to imaginatively discern various possibilities for acting within a given situation and to envision the potential help and harm that are likely to result from a given action."[14] Understanding that it is narrow-mindedness, fantasy, or self-deception which can make us dismiss possibilities that might make our lives better or to pursue unsuitable possibilities that can make our lives worse, allows us to take corrective action. The key is to discern the difference, which can depend on the amount of control we have over possibilities. Our moral imagination enlarges the field of possibilities beyond what our culture provides. Of course, some

---

[13] Kekes, John. Moral Imagination, Freedom and the Humanities. American Philosophical Quarterly. Vol. 28, No.2 (April, 1991), p.109.
[14] Johnson, p.202.

human possibilities ought not to be explored. Some limits are necessary.[15]

From a moral perspective, our imagination engages our abilities to empathize with different people. Using metaphors, imagery, and storytelling all assist us in being able to sympathize and communicate in a caring way with each other about our shared experiences. They enable us to reflect on the moral context of a situation and see how actions might be right in one context and wrong in another. To be able to imagine how something that has happened to another, good or bad, can happen to us, and what it will feel like, is part of this. Engaging our moral imagination can lead us to see that there is not always one right answer. A variety of different possibilities can exist in a given situation, and recognizing them permits us to uncover possible consequences we had not seen or thought of before.[16] This method of thinking is beautifully reflected in the North American Natives' ethos of imagining how a decision today will impact the lives of their tribe seven generations from now. This is how a caring imagination truly works, for it considers not just those alive today but those not yet born who will inherit a world that we created today for them, for either good or bad.

Perhaps the wisdom of Rudolf Steiner is particularly helpful in understanding moral imagination and its role for leaders of the light in the 21st century. Steiner maintained that to be a moral and ethical individual needs imagination. The individual who is a free spirit uses moral imagination to envision ethical goals. An ethical deed is based on an ethical principle. The problem is that ethical principles are universal in nature and do not give specific instructions on how to act in a given situation. Imagination is needed to creatively translate an ethical principle

---

[15] Kekes, p.110.
[16] Ladkin, pp. 99-100.

into a goal of action. This creative ability is called moral imagination. A picture is formed in the mind of the action that will be carried out. This is how we actualize our ideals into real life. The moment an impulse to action is present in universal conceptual form, for example, you should do good to your fellow human beings! You should live in a way that ensures good health! In each particular case, the concrete idea of action must first be found. While principles are abstract, concrete ideas are practical and concerned with actual things. Unfree spirits look for concrete ideas in their past experience. They recall what someone else has done or recommended in a similar situation or what God has commanded to be done. A free spirit does not receive their ideas from others, but instead makes an original decision. The free spirit has no role model to imitate and does not obey the will of others. So, it is necessary for the free spirit to originate a new concrete idea that will become the goal of action. Concrete ideas are formed by us by means of the imagination. The free spirit needs moral imagination in order to assert himself or herself in the world. Thus, moral imagination is the source of the free spirit in action.

In fact, only people with moral imagination, according to Steiner, are morally productive. Those who merely preach morality, people who merely devise codes of ethics without the ability to condense them into concrete ideas, are morally unproductive. They are like the art critic who can explain very competently what a good work of art should be like, but he himself is incapable of achieving the slightest artistic production.

REFERENCES

de Waal, Frans. *The Age of Empathy: Nature's Lessons for a Kinder Society*. New York: McClelland & Stewart, 2009.

Ladkin, Donna. *Mastering the Ethical Dimension of Organizations: A Self-Reflective Guide to Developing Ethical Astuteness*. Cheltenham, UK: Edward Elgar, 2015.

Johnson, Mark. "Imagination in Moral Judgment." *Philosophy and Phenomenological Research*. Dec. 1985, Vol. 46, No. 2. pp. 265-280.

Johnson, Mark. *Moral Imagination: Implications of Cognitive Science for Ethics*. Chicago: The University of Chicago Press, 1993.

Kekes, John. "Moral Imagination, Freedom and the Humanities." *American Philosophical Quarterly*. April, 1991, Vol. 28, No. 2, pp 101-111.

Nussbaum, Martha C. *Love's Knowledge: Essays on Philosophy and Literature*. Oxford: Oxford University Press, 1990.

Smith, Adam. *Theory of Moral Sentiments*. New York: Penguin Books. 2009 (originally published 1790).

Werhane, Patricia H. "Moral Imagination and the Search for Ethical Decision-Making in Management." *Business Quarterly*.

Vol 8, Issue S1 (The Ruffin Series Special Issue, No.1) 1998, pp. 75-98.

Chapter Eight

Conclusion

"The Shroud of the Dark Side has fallen."
Yoda (Star Wars, Episode 2)

The title of this work refers to a struggle between "Light Leaders" or light workers and those leaders and workers on the 'dark side'. Many of the thoughts expressed here sadly point to the predominance of the latter. The magnitude of evil permeating the planet at this time is staggering. This book is not about rainbows and unicorns but is meant to do a reality-based analysis and provide a foundation of hope and change for the future. The predictive words of Yoda can be interpreted in one or two ways. One, the shroud has fallen over humans' eyes so they cannot see the evil in their midst. Or two, the shroud has fallen away, and now humans can see the darkness and evil that has engulfed them. It's as if those trapped in Plato's cave have emerged and can finally see clearly in the light of day. It is this interpretation that is endorsed here as it offers us a new hope for a different, more spiritual world. In other words, the veil at long last has lifted or fallen away. We are now living in the age of transparency and revelation. We have an opportunity that many people have longed for to make a new world, if we have the courage to do it.

The writer and teacher Gary Zuhav has summed up the world that leaders of the light and light workers will have to deal with and what he deems its causation, namely the pursuit of external power and its solution, the emergence of the 'universal human':

The world we have inherited from five-sensory humanity is filled with painful consequences of pursuing external power. Pursuit of external power has destroyed entire species and is destroying more. Seas surge through coastal cities, inextinguishable fires burn huge forests, air is foul, water is worse, glaciers melt, and ice disappears from the Earth's poles. Hurricanes are more frequent and intense, temperatures skyrocket or plunge. Food supplies shrink. Wars proliferate. Poverty, disease, starvation, and thirst are everywhere and spreading. Nuclear war looms. All because of pursuing external power. Callousness covers the land. The rich take refuge behind police, and the poor despair or revolt.

Universal Humans see these things clearly and address them directly. They replace callousness with compassion, conquest with cocreativity, and despair of distance from one another with the joy of uniting. They commit themselves to Life. They commit their actions to Life. They commit their lives to Life. They create social structures to support Life. They act and speak with beneficence and the unlimited power of their intentions of love. They cultivate their love of Life, focus their love of Life, and consciously apply their love of Life to the flowering of the human species…They are the flowering of the human species.[1]

There are many developments and forces that have created the world we now live in. This work is hardly a definitive analysis of all of them. Two, however, stand out and have received attention in this work: the emergence and control of psychopaths, and two, the mind 'virus' they carry and have infected human societies with. So many

---

[1] Gary Zuhav, <u>Universal Human</u> (Astria Paperback, New York, 2021), p.233.

humans have succumbed and given their power away to a class of predators and parasites who have ruled the roost and kept humans trapped in a 3D, five-sensory world. Only a handful of "rulers" were 'leaders' of the Light. One was Marcus Aurelius, a Roman Emperor, and another was Emperor Asoke of India in the third century BC. Both of these men experienced wars and bloodshed and yet could still envision a peaceful and harmonious world. They came close to being a "Philosopher King" that Plato spoke of. They may not have been able to foresee a 4D world, but it would have been a good start in that direction.

At this date, it is clear to many that we are living through a time of great 'anomie'. By that, one means a social condition defined by an uprooting or breakdown of moral values, standards, ideals, or guidelines for individuals to follow. Conflicting belief systems and the breakdown of social bonds between an individual and the community are evident on every continent.[2] So many human societies are disintegrating. Perhaps humanity is going through a period of gestation, out of which a new civilization will be birthed. Though there are many possible forms this new civilization will look like, two very distinct pathways can be recognized. One path is that of centralization, with more and more power and wealth focused around and concentrated in fewer and fewer people. Paving the road to centralization are the transhumanist technocrats with their technological control fixes, computers, robots, nano-technology, artificial intelligence, i.e., the singularity, and the internet of all things. The oligarchic structure of so many governments and economies have created a base from which this transhumanist technocracy can easily emerge, driven and motivated by the elites insane drive for complete control. In the thinking of the World Economic Forum, it will be a world with one world

---

[2] Wikepedia

government, one world military, one world economy, and even one world religion where people will eat bugs, own nothing, and be happy. This is the dystopian future so many globalists are advocating.

From a spiritual point of view, what is behind this development is a lack of reverence. A reverent person and society are essentially spiritual, and to quote Gary Zuhav, there is currently no place for spirituality within science, politics, business, or academia. Multisensory humans understand, live, and evoke reverence. A multisensory human, a reverent businessman or businesswoman, is a person who infuses a new energy into the archetype of entrepreneur, shifting it from a dynamic that is motivated by profits that are generated by serving others to a dynamic of serving others that is made possible by profits. A reverent politician is a person who challenges the concept of external power and brings to the political arena the concerns of the heart. Therefore, the decision to approach Life with reverence means acting and thinking as a spiritual person in a world that does not recognize spirit, and means moving consciously toward the perceptions of the multisensory human.[3] A multisensory personality evolves out of a sense of richness and fullness and intimacy of being. It creates compassion and kindness. Without reverence, without the perception of the holiness of all things, the world becomes cold and barren, mechanical and random at the same time, and this creates experiences of alienation and acts of violence. In essence, it is not natural for us to live without reverence, because this separates us from the basic energy of the soul.[4] But it is hard not to conclude that this is exactly where a technological, technocratic dystopia ends up.

Undermining spiritual reverence is another insidious force, for behind the curtain or shroud is a surreptitious and hidden power. It is

---

[3] Gary Zuhav, The Seat of the Soul (Simon and Shuster, 2014), pp. 40-41.
[4] Ibid. p. 41.

used to control people without their conscious awareness. It is a mind virus, a mass group consciousness, or mass entrainment psychosis. It uses propaganda, the media, progressive education, and brain-washed corrupt politicians and bureaucrats to control the thinking and values of people. The indigenous peoples refer to it as *wetiko*, the gnostics as archons, Rudolf Steiner as Ahriman, and Christians as devils and demons. To modern advocates of scientific materialism, these invisible forces or entities are delusions. It is submitted here that it is these very invisible entities that have infested the minds of so many past and present "rulers". One can see this in the prevalence of so many psychopaths and sociopaths among their ranks. This can include anyone who has done very little work on the unlit part of their ego. What these entities unleash is felt and experienced by humans as fear, anger, violence, hatred, and other negative expressions that allow psychopathic rulers to control and triumph. Humans caught by it live in a fight-or-flight mode.

Humanity's inability to acknowledge these entities stems from its psychic frailness to see and comprehend the metaphysical noumenal. Reason alone cannot grasp it. A five-sensory human can only really have phenomenal experiences. A multisensory human who has done the inner work will develop a higher consciousness and awareness and will not be so limited.

A different path forward to a 5D world will be one that leads to decentralization and localization of every aspect of human life. Our farming will be locally owned, organic, and relying on the principles of regenerative agriculture and not massive, corporate, soil-depleting, monoculture farms. The emphasis will be on producing and growing nutritional, non-chemically altered or enhanced crops, and not agribusinesses that put profits first and human health second. Political institutions, monetary exchange systems even religious institutions will be localized. This will make all of these human activities more democratic and accountable. Like fractals, our light workers will become the new "leaders" as leadership will be the task and responsibility of every human. Their lives will be governed by an ancient Hopi saying that humans will learn to be good to each other and not to look beyond themselves for the leader.[5] The long-awaited appearance and recognition of the worth of servant leadership will quietly unfold. Servant leaders are not people ruled by their egos or focused on control, dominance, and power. They aspire to serve others first and to put the growth of others as a priority. Do their followers become healthier, wiser, freer, more autonomous, and more likely themselves to become servants?[6] This will be the face of 5D leadership.

One cannot envision a 5D world without considering its political dimensions. Using the framework of government and the cycle of constitutional development contemplated by Plato, Polybius, Xenophon, and others thousands of years ago, one can see a framework for its potential expression. On the positive side are democracy, aristocracy, and monarchy. They might well be activated in a mixed way so that there are elements of each and a separation of powers, resulting in balances of power, and institutional checks to prevent aggregations that can result in a tyranny. These ancient philosophers also saw how each of these states could degenerate to its negative expression: ochlocracy (mob rule), oligarchy, and tranny. Modern history illustrates that a positive mixed constitutional format, advocated by Montesquieu, Locke, Machiavelli, and America's founding fathers, Madison, Jay, Hamilton, Franklin, and others, have best stood the test of time. The focus here is a separation of power that prevents power from being concentrated and exclusive. What that will look like in a 5D world will likely be a decentralized, inclusive one, where freedoms, power, energy, and material benefits

---

[5] Gary Zuhav, Universal Human (Simon and Schuster, 2021), p.232.
[6] Robert K. Greenleaf, The Servant as Leader (The Robert K. Greenleaf Center, 1991), p.7.

are the inheritance of everyone. It will be a society with some form of true participatory democracy. The only modern state that comes close in some ways to this is Switzerland.

It might be assumed, wrongly, that this 5D world will become a Marxist, communist state with all the evils and horrendous outcomes that communism brought humanity in the twentieth century. A communist state can only devolve out of the constitutional paradigm already noted, especially its negative expressions. It became the God that failed. Its latest incarnation is the 'Great Reset.' As Gregg Braden has put it in describing the "Great Reset", "it's a world that replaces our ideas and values, such as individuality, uniqueness, innovation, and self-reliance, with a muted and homogenous society that is viewed as fair and equal for all. The problem is that what's thought of as fair and equal by some, particularly those in power, is a world in which others of us have lost so many of our hard-won freedoms. It's a world where speech, ideas, and information are controlled. They have to be so new that innovations and options that threaten the status quo are not known or made available. Rather than the traditional and time-honored world of localized living that has proven to be healthy, sustainable, and viable for millennia, the Great Reset world would be one of centralized power, centralized control, centralized resources, and sameness, all regulated using a new wave of surveillance technology and "smart" systems."[7] However, it is submitted here that new forms of self-government will emerge based on fractal and servant leadership modalities and values. Obviously, such states can only hope to emerge when humans are more self-reliant, productive, independent thinking and spiritually aware. Moreover, a great many humans will have to step up and become leaders themselves. This means they will deliberately

---

[7] Gregg Braden, <u>Pure Human: The Hidden Truth of Our Divinity, Power, and Destiny</u> (Hay House LLC, 2025), p.177.

and consciously choose to be sovereign and free individuals who look within for leadership capabilities, rather than surrender their sovereignty to external sources. The thought of becoming a slave dependent upon a monarch, government, or corporation will be abhorrent to them.

At this point, it is worth repeating what Albert Einstein supposedly once said, "You cannot solve problems with the same thinking that created them." This means that human spiritual, social, and material values will have to massively transform to usher in the Age of Great Awakening. There are many signs that this is already happening, though to some advanced souls, it is happening at a glacial pace. Here are some of the changes that must manifest in order for there to be a spiritual foundation of a new age. Firstly, our pollutant-generating energy systems will have to rendered obsolete as were coal mines and steam engines centuries ago. Many futurists and gifted scientists, and engineers have shown and proven that the technological means to do this already exist: radiant energy, zero point energy, anti-matter, and anti-gravity propulsion systems, nuclear fusion, plasma technologies, and much more. The current ruling elites have suppressed these technological breakthroughs in order to preserve their wealth and power. Thousands of patents are frozen because they are a threat to "national security." This suppression has not only obstructed human evolution but has actively and consciously endangered all life on the planet. They must be removed quickly, peacefully, if possible.

A second profound change must occur, and that is the end of our allopathic medical system. We have made "gods" out of men and women in white coats with stethoscopes who are trained in pathology and disease but know very little about how to live healthy, vital, mentally balanced lives. They are accustomed to learning about life through the study of dead matter: carcasses and corpses. They are trained to offer a small handful of primitive and deadly cures: drugs, surgery, chemo and radiation. All of these are financed and supported by Big Pharma profit-driven industries that kill far more people than they can ever cure. Worse, they have slammed the door on so many alternative forms of medicine, such as acupuncture, homeopathy, naturopathy, aromatherapy, herbs, Ayurveda, breathwork, Traditional Chinese Medicine, German New Medicine, mindful meditation, and countless other viable expressions of health preservation that have been used for hundreds of years by indigenous peoples. Most egregiously, they have stripped humans of their god given natural abilities to heal themselves. And it is this human trait that will someday soon be rediscovered. It will replace most of the allopathic interventions mentioned. Humans will remember how to access their higher multidimensional selves and cure themselves of most of their physical ailments without surgery, radiation, or chemo by mentally healing past traumas. A century from now, those will be seen as useless as blood-letting and the use of leeches in centuries past. Work in this area has really only just begun, as souls are emerging from 4D dimensional thinking to 5D.

A third great change will be needed for a 5D world to thrive, and that is the creation of viable, sustainable food and shelter for humans. A revolution in agriculture will be based on regenerative farming, with organic crops. It will mean an end to giant monoculture farming that is profit-driven, soil-depleting, polluting, and health-destroying. Farming will return to local communities, and people will learn how to grow their own food again. Fortunately, signs of this development are already emerging.

Four, people will recognize, and awaken, to the reality that this planet's weather has been weaponized by a very small percentage of the population, a truly evil cabal, that is determined to depopulate the planet not only of humans but destroy all carbon-based forms of life. The elites' control of mass media, education, the military, governments, and large private global corporations have precluded and prevented an awakening of the masses who are trapped in a mass mind consciousness. Many of their theories of planetary climate change, solar emissions, and excessive carbon dioxide levels are bogus and based on false science. Yet so many humans tolerate the spraying of our skies with chemtrails as harmless, despite the scientific evidence that they are being sprayed with aluminum, barium, strontium, sulfur dioxide, sulphate aerosols, lipid nanoparticles, graphene oxide, and more in the stratosphere. Dane Wigginton and his courageous work at geoengineeringwatch.org has done more than anyone to expose this travesty, planetary devastation, and catastrophic natural outcomes. He has clearly shown that mankind's arrogant attempt to control and rule the weather, i.e., nature, is not only futile but suicidal. It reminds one of the Biblical story of Nimrod's Tower of Babel. And we know how that one ended.

Lastly, from a practical perspective, some significant level of transformation will be needed for rewarding, exchanging people's creative efforts and energy. Our current debt-based monetary systems are on the verge of collapsing. Never before has there been so much money yet also so much artificial scarcity. People everywhere feel betrayed by their economic and political systems and the elites who have profited from them. They are, in essence, a self-appointed ruling class that puts as much power as it can in the hands of a privileged few. Here, a quote from Einstein is particularly relevant: "The most powerful force in the universe is compound interest." The changes made in this area, a subject so vast as to be beyond the scope of this work, will have a massive impact on humanity and its spiritual evolution.[8] But until a stable, equitable, and morally justifiable financial order is created, no 5D world can ever exist for long.

----

[8] To understand the financial foundation that our world rests on today, one could start by reading Edward Griffin's The Creature from Jekyll Island, and Carroll Quigley's Tragedy and Hope: A History of the World in Our Time.

What this new financial order will look like is anyone's guess at this time. It could be entirely electronic, or an exchange of valuable commodities, digital token sticks, new methods and technologies of measuring and disbursing energy, or perhaps a new form of paper of plastic currency. Whatever form it takes, this new financial order must produce a certain level of affluence that allows enough people to live above a 3D bare subsistence level. Money or its substitute will be allowed to flow and circulate, and not be hoarded. If there is sufficient abundance, then there would be no need to hoard it. Banks will act as trustees responsible to the public at large, not a small group of private or powerful shareholders or a banking cartel. Private banking cartels will have to be outlawed. A new financial system will not be one that attempts to monetize, tokenize, or digitalize externalities like water, the air we breathe, sunlight, bee pollination, photosynthesis, forests, or any other natural process.

Though it may be hard for people in the West today to fully appreciate a life of poverty in which all one's time and energy is consumed with simply trying to survive, such a life is not one that can produce a human race that can live at a 5D spiritual level. Again, this will not be a communist state, but one that allows individuals to rise and accumulate wealth, provided they do not infringe or steal from others. At the end of the day, we must recognize that we cannot get to where we dream of being tomorrow unless we change our thinking today. Much of our thinking today is posed to move in the direction of a centralized and private banking-dominated structure, top-down controlled and hierarchical, whether you call it communism or capitalism. Another path that could be taken would be one that is decentralized, entrepreneurial, laissez-faire, bottom-up, libertarian, with multiple methods of exchange. Such a state could be based on a 'spontaneous order.' However, that would require an invisible "policeman" to ensure that human greed, selfishness, and profit-taking do not devour everything human and natural. Our moral capacities, if sufficiently transformed, could accomplish this as discussed in the chapter, "The Ethics and Moral Foundation of a 5th Dimensional World." But only a significant change in human consciousness that precedes it can ever hope to achieve it in a lasting way. Currently, human consciousness is not anywhere near a state in which humanity can exist without some form of external government.

It needs to be stressed here again that all of the foregoing challenges, or impediments, to the emergence of a 5D world will require an uplifting of human consciousness. In order for that to happen, humans will have to do the difficult 'shadow work' and deal with their traumas that have weakened them. This means numerous, multiple actions, not those of just a few brave artists, writers, scientists who understand quantum physics, or poets who have become balanced, multisensory, and authentic beings. Gary Zukav refers to this as the emergence of a 'universal human': "You cannot leap from ignorance into Universal Humanity in a single bound. You must create authentic power. You must develop emotional awareness, practice responsible choice, and consult your intuition. Most important, you must create the ability to speak and act with love, even while frightened parts of your personality demand to speak and act from fear."[9] People will learn to look within for happiness and not rely on external power and materiality. In doing so, they will become multisensory. That is what Zuhav means by authentic power. It will also mean that people will need to reject the past and embrace a new future, with a new narrative. Obviously, given our current paradigm, it will take time to turn eight billion people around.

Unhappily, the path forward contemplated here appears long, slow, and arduous, taking decades or centuries. But it is not the only

----

[9] Gary Zuhav, p. 275.

path that humanity may take. It might be possible to change our destiny in a matter of a few generations. How? Perhaps nature can show us. Think of a large school of thousands of fish or birds swimming or flying together as a collective. Suddenly, and spontaneously, they change directions completely. What happened? Did they collectively communicate the change, or is it just random? Another example from nature is the 100th monkey effect, which consists of the unconscious transference of knowledge or awareness throughout an entire species. It starts with the learning of a new skill of just one monkey. In other words, once a certain number of individual monkeys learn a new idea, skill, or action, it bypasses physical barriers and jumps from monkey mind to monkeys on different islands who have not been in the physical presence of the first monkeys. It is an increase and a leap in consciousness. Does it always take 100 to reach the tipping point to shift the balance into a new paradigm? How many humans will it take, 300 million or three billion, to reach a tipping point and shift our collective human consciousness? Is it possible we are closer to this point right now, and the shift into a 5D dimension is very near? One can be optimistic and hopeful.

In concluding, a few words need to be said about the real threat and nemesis to an emerging 5D world. Parts of this work have referred to it. This is technocracy, and in the words of one futurist, Patrick M. Wood, it is the Trojan horse of global transformation and world order.[10] It has been said that humanity at this moment is finally leaving a dark age, the Kala Yuga, and is about to enter a new age of light, the Age of Aquarius. There are, however, some dark clouds that Gregg Braden has put in the following words: "Our best minds have said unless we change

---

[10] Patrick M. Wood is the author of <u>Technocracy Rising: The Trojan Horse of Global Transformation</u>, and <u>Technocracy: The Hard Road to World Order</u>. Another author who has written on this subject is Daniel Estulin, author of <u>Trans Evolution: The Coming Age of Human Deconstruction.</u>

our thinking and unless we change the path we are on, within about 5 years there will be very few pure humans remaining on the planet today. When you meet someone in a store, you will be talking to some form of hybrid or machine. There is a move to replace our biology with technology: computer chips in the brain, chemicals in the blood, sensors, RFID microchips, sensors, and AI." This will be the new Singularity (internet of things/bodies) when machines become 'conscious' and AI technical intelligence will exceed human intelligence with quantum computing and quantum intelligence. By 2029, it is believed that AI will reach human intelligence, and by 2045, the completion of the merger of AI and the human body will be attained. This vision is a dystopian horror story that many tech billionaires are so oblivious to, nor care about, if they could appreciate the dark side of their psychopathic intentions. Their dreams will only lead to the strengthening of the 3rd Dimension and encasing it in an electronic prison.

Another vision of the future is possible, however, that contradicts the darkness of the myopic technocrats' fantasies. No matter how dark you see certain periods of history in the past, such as in the Dark Ages, humanity's will and spirit to survive and prosper has always prevailed. Humans are erroneously presumed to be selfish, governed primarily by self-interest. In truth, as Rutger Bregmen has pointed out in Humankind: A Hopeful History, humans are hardwired for kindness, geared toward cooperation rather than competition, and more inclined to trust rather than distrust one another. Without these traits, humanity would have gone extinct thousands of years ago. We are conscious, spiritual beings. And it is these traits that will prevail over the technocrats' fascist and totalitarian imaginary fantasies.

No matter how powerful computers and AI become, they will forever lack a numinous quality. This refers to the ability to sense an invisible presence or force which, when experienced, has the ability to arouse an alteration of consciousness with emotional value. It is an expression of real intelligence necessitating a consciousness that no machine will ever possess. People use technology to make life more convenient, not more human or spiritual. The qualities that make us unique as a species are empathy, compassion, courage, love, intuition, passion, and imagination. They can never come from a machine or an AI program. This new iteration of humanity will someday be known as Homo Spiritus. Humans will be multi-sensory, though it will take several generations for this to truly emerge. They will, by nature, be light leaders and will be prolific. They will be left and right brain balanced, not left-brain dominant. They will have done their shadow work. They will have made the lonely inner journey to become authentic beings, and not narcissistic actors strutting on a stage or in front of a camera.

In closing, it seems most appropriate to call upon the eloquence of Stuart Wilde, expressing what a 5D world will look like:

> Within mankind, there is a long-forgotten dream. It is a dream of a time when purity of spirit ruled the earth, when love truly supported mankind, when each had time to evolve as he or she wished, a time when the individuality of self was revered; a time when there were no governments, no religions, no rules or regulations, for each person understood his responsibility to others and there was no infringement or mass thinking or forced conformity. There was a spontaneous enlightenment, instinctive creativity, and you heard the laughter of a man having fun.

Through your knowledge and power, that time will return. Not for all mankind, but for you and those who will be attracted to individuals such as you, who are expressing powerfully. For, in the darkest times, the Force always provides a spark of light, and that light is carried by a few and later passes to others.

Your heritage, your life's heroic goal, is to work upon yourself to the point where the Force grants you the right to carry its light. And when you have done so for a while, you will earn the right to go do other things. You will look back at the world and you will hear a funny bag of bones with toothpick legs go "tweet," and somewhere a man will laugh in an atmosphere of total calm, and you will be able to say to yourself, "I helped create that."

And you will know what is meant by the "Golden Age."[11]

Such an age, the Age of Homo Spiritus, will only come when more humans courageously live as George Bernard Shaw once put it: "Some men see things as they are and ask why, others dream things that never were and ask why not."

> *"A dream you dream alone is only a dream.*
> *A dream you dream together is reality."*
>
> *– John Lennon.*

---

[11] Stuart Wilde, The Force (White Dove International , Inc., Taos NM, 1984), pp. 74-75.

REFERENCES

Braden, Gregg. Pure Human: The Hidden Truth of Our Divinity, Power, and Destiny. Hay House LLC, 2025.

Estulin, Daniel. TransEvolution: The Coming Age of Human Deconstruction. Walterville, OR: Trine Day, 2014.

Greenleaf, Robert K. The Servant as Leader. Indianapolis, IN: Robert K. Greenleaf Center, 1991.

Griffin, G.Edward. The Creature from Jekyll Island. Westlake Village, CA: American Media, 1998.

Quigley, Carroll. Tragedy and Hope: A History of the World in Our Time. New York: The Macmillan Company, 1966.

Wilde, Stuart. The Force. Taos, NM; White Dove International, 1984.

Wood, Patrick M. Technocracy Rising: The Trojan Horse of Global Transformation. Mesa, AZ: Coherent Press, 2015.

Zukav, Gary. The Seat of the Soul. New York: Simon& Schuster, 1989.

Zukav, Gary. Spiritual Partnership: The Journey to Authentic Power. New York: HarperCollins, 2010.

Zukav, Gary. Universal Human. New York: Simon & Schuster, 2021.

About The Author

Mr. Valeri is a retired college instructor, business consultant, and lawyer. His academic background includes a B.A. (Honours) from Carleton University, an LL.B / J.D. from the University of Ottawa, and. an M.B.A. from the University of Ottawa, and a Ph.D. (With Distinction) from Greenleaf University (online). He is the author of The Origins of Servant Leadership; Servant Leadership's Past and Potential Future (2007).

His work experience includes private practice in law, corporate counsel in industry, service with Canada's Federal Government, and work as a college instructor for twenty-five years at a college in British Columbia, Canada.